Stewards of God's Delight

Stewards of God's Delight

Becoming Priests of the New Creation

Mark Clavier

Foreword by
Barry Morgan

CASCADE *Books* • Eugene, Oregon

STEWARDS OF GOD'S DELIGHT
Becoming Priests of the New Creation

Cascade Books
An Imprint of Wipf and Stock Publishers
199 W. 8th Ave., Suite 3
Eugene, OR 97401

www.wipfandstock.com

ISBN 13: 978-1-4982-2543-4

Cataloguing-in-Publication Data

Clavier, Mark.

Stewards of God's delight : becoming priests of the new creation / Mark
Clavier; foreword by Barry Morgan.

xvi + 100 p. ; 22 cm. Includes bibliographical references.

ISBN 13: 978-1-4982-2543-4

1. Vocation Christianity. 2. Spiritual life Christianity. 3. Theology study
and teaching. I. Title.

BV4740 .C50 2016

Manufactured in the USA.   12/11/2015

I dedicate this book to all the men and women in whose formation for ministry I've played some part. Very little fills me with more delight than to be present at the ordination or licensing of people whom I've come to know and (usually) love as they prepared for the ministry. Deep ministerial formation is sadly becoming rarer as programs are scaled back and residential training ended. For that reason (among many others), I consider it a privilege to have experienced such prayerful, intimate, and studious communities and to have shared with the students a vision of the ministry that I hope has helped to sustain them in their subsequent vocations. I wrote hardly a page of this book without them uppermost in mind.

Contents

Foreword

THIS BOOK, BASED ON talks given to those about to be ordained, is far more wide-ranging and all encompassing than the usual books on this subject. That is because the author places the work of the ordained firmly in the context of the whole created order rather than more narrowly in the church, since the world is the sphere of God's operation since he created it and because of his love for it sent Jesus to redeem it. The task of the ordained ministry therefore is not to save people from this "naughty world," as the Prayer Book has it, so that they might go to heaven, but to offer thanks for that creation and to minister to every living thing within it. Nor is ministry restricted to those who are ordained but consists of all God's people. The task of all of us therefore is to offer God on the world's behalf the praise it has forgotten how to express. Because every aspect of life is therefore of concern to God there can be no separation of the holy from the ordinary, the religious from the secular—it all bears the Creator's signature.

These chapters are bracing, drawing richly from the author's ministerial, academic, and life experience on both sides of the pond, marked by a homely directness seasoned with substantial and appropriate quotations from a wide-ranging collection of saints, authors, and scholars. More than this, his talks have an originality where he challenges his hearers to focus their ministry in the light of God's generosity, freedom, delight, and love. Mark's big idea is seeing the minister as someone who is freed up to delight in the beauty of creation, a delight that is contagious, spilling over to benefit all those caught up in the ministry. It is a realistic delight, for all too often noticing and celebrating beauty has its high price: after all, merely driving to a national park leaves its destructive carbon footprint. Humankind may be the only creature both to notice and be oblivious to beauty, and is the only creature aware of its fallen nature, its dissonance, disconnection, and disharmony with the natural and beautiful order, often willfully conspiring in its exploitation and destruction, a multiple crucifixion. The priest stands and aches with Christ in such places, but does not stop there, instead directing our gaze towards Easter, with its high gospel of restoration and resurrection, that nothing is beyond Christ's risen touch, bringing glorious life and harmony even out of death and destruction.

Drawing on St. Augustine, Mark boldly claims that there is no delight without love. In his final chapter he sets out the four ladder-like rungs of perceiving love in Bernard of Clairvaux's *On Loving God*. He gives clear examples of how they can be applied to ministry, turning around even the most dire and unpromising situations, ending the book on a very practical high. Mark's own enchantment with the whole of creation comes across loud and clear on every page, enabling his readers to realign themselves and embrace the delight that they may have missed for too long.

Dr. Barry Morgan

Archbishop of Wales

Preface

THIS BOOK AROSE OUT of a series of talks I gave in June 2014 during a retreat for a group of men and women about to be ordained in the Church in Wales. Despite the initial, all-too-typical wet Welsh weather, it was a week I will long treasure. Not only did I get to spend time in teaching, prayer, and fellowship with a remarkable group of people but I also had time to hike along the Pembrokeshire Coastal Path above the crashing waves of the Irish Sea, and to preach in the ancient Cathedral of St. David's, the origins of which go back to sixth century. I can think of few other occasions that have allowed me to combine my favorite activities of teaching, preaching, praying, and going for long walks. Perhaps happiest of all, the invitation gave me a reason finally to tie together the two things that have probably most influenced my own faith: nearly twenty years of priestly ministry within the Anglican tradition and over six years of thinking hard about the idea of delight. I can genuinely say that before I composed my talks I'd never stopped to reflect upon and try to integrate these two strands of my experience as a Christian.

I did not at the time have any intention of turning those talks into a book. But the appreciative responses of those ordinands and their apparent unfamiliarity with so much of what I was saying planted the idea that such a book might not be unwelcome. Subsequently, as I became involved in developing new schemes for ministerial formation and observed the often heated debate about how to train clergy and lay ministers, I became increasingly convinced that I did, in fact, need to write this book. There are at least three reasons why I believe this (other than, of course, the conceit required for thinking one's own musings worthy of other people's time):

First, we're now well into the midst of a period of what I call ecclesial amnesia. By that I mean that the church is forgetting about what it is. Just as wider society has broken loose from many of its historical and cultural roots, so too has the church lost sight of much that once fed and watered it. Many Christians have only a minimal familiarity with the Bible. Church history is rarely emphasized in ministry training or in the teaching programs of local congregations. Practices that once characterized worship or communities of Christians have fallen into disuse. Certainly, the loss of some of these practices and customs is neither manifestly bad nor unprecedented. Customs change with the times. At the same time, the church arguably hasn't experienced such a cultural sea change since the Reformation and it took some Protestant churches generations to recover some of the good that was lost. I can't help but wonder what goods we are losing now.

Second, with this ecclesial amnesia has come a loss of a rich ministerial identity. So much of our language about the ministry these days hardly touches upon the great tradition as found, for example, in Gregory Nazienzen, Augustine of Hippo, Gregory the Great, and George Herbert. Instead, we are presented with a dizzying array of rationalized models for ministry that look not so much to tradition or even Scripture as they do to the business world and the expanding field of management theory and technique. Admittedly, there is a great deal of practical know-how in these models that can do much to make the conduct of the ministry more efficient. But I suspect that I'm not the only one who finds their presentation of the Christian ministry singularly uninspiring. They may be wonderful from the viewpoint of organizational theory, but the way they are detached from an identifiable Christian tradition is disturbing. It's like rationalizing romantic relationships or getting parents to conform to a scientific approach to parenthood that neglects family traditions and relationships. I'm sure with either of these examples one might develop an efficient alternative to traditional approaches but not without the loss of charm, rooted-ness, and a bit of fun.

Finally, I think we have entered an age when our increasingly virtual, computerized experience of life has begun to reshape our sense of connection with the world. More and more, I hear language that suggests that our true selves are like software and our bodies like hardware. I suspect a great many people think of their true selves as being somehow detached from their bodies, which are seen as being mainly useful canvasses for advertising our true selves (e.g., through fashion, tattoos, plastic surgery, etc.) or obstacles that need to be overcome (e.g., through pharmaceuticals). Similarly, in film, computer games, and the like, we are presented with ideal worlds on a level never experienced before and this can give us a stronger sense of freedom than we are likely to experience in the real world—I will never bowl the scores in real life that I do on my son's Wii. For a great many people in Western society, these fabricated worlds are the ones they inhabit and where they feel most at home. Now, I don't think people believe that in the real world they can become like people in films or games, but I do think these platforms enhance the belief that we can be and do whatever we like; that we are in effect enfleshed avatars. And so, we intuitively believe that we should be able to choose, even design, our own identities—that's the state most familiar to us—and we believe this firmly enough to pour money and resources into breaking down social, physical, and ecological barriers to this freedom. In response, the world groans.

When I sat down to begin writing this book, therefore, I wanted to accomplish three things. First, I wanted to present an inspiring and appealing vision of the Christian vision that savors of heaven but is firmly rooted in creation. If you detect in my presentation something of the mythic, perhaps even of fairy tales, then I've achieved my goal. This book is a deliberate attempt to re-enchant the ministry. Now, I hope I've done this in a way that avoids impractical idealism or sentimentalism; at the same time, I believe strongly that there is a romance to the Christian ministry that by its very nature eludes being systematized.

Second, I wanted to present my vision in conversation with some of the great Christian thinkers whose thought has enriched my own ministry and theological outlook. In other words, I wanted to show how my vision isn't just mine but is one that draws nourishment from Scripture and the church throughout the centuries. I have gone out of my way to include a variety of great theologians, authors, and poets who seem to me to have a shared appreciation of God, creation, and humanity's place in the world. If you find fault with my approach to the ministry, I hope you may at least encounter some unfamiliar Christian voices and be inspired to discover them further for yourself.

Finally, I thought it was important to connect this vision with the actual ministry in a way that people might find useful. Achieving this last goal was difficult because it required a careful balancing act between being suggestive in practical ways without becoming too prescriptive. It isn't my intention to tell readers how they should conduct their ministry. Despite this, too often I felt as though I were implying that I'm an expert at ministerial practice, which I most certainly am not. While I have over sixteen years of ministerial experience in churches in both America and Great Britain, and pray that I've picked up a few insights along the way, I believe the ministry by its very nature is not tameable. One reason for this is that whether we're ordained or lay, we are never more than assistant ministers; Christ himself always remains the chief minister who leads the way. With that in mind, my final task is offered in the hope that my own suggestions and reflection might spark some fruitful ideas for your ministry in your own context. They are conversation starters and in no way the last word.

Acknowledgments

IN A WORK SUCH as this that draws on not only past experience but also ideas encountered in lectures, half-forgotten conversations, sermons, and long discussions with friends, it's impossible to acknowledge everyone who deserves to be. But one of the delights of friendship is that conversations and views often merge into one another over time as we experience—to our joy and bemusement—living in each other's heads. My friends and teachers know who they are and may recognize echoes of their own voices in this book. I hope they will take it as read that I'm thankful for the countless ways they've influenced me and my thoughts for the better.

Having said that, there are people who do deserve particular mention either for providing the occasion for writing this book or for directly shaping my thinking. First, I'd like to thank Prof. Carol Harrison and Dr. Giles Gasper, who together introduced me to the serious study of Augustine and medieval theologians. Like Beatrice with Dante, they guided me into a world I hardly knew existed and that has ever since filled me with wonder. I also owe a debt of gratitude to the Rev. Canon Dr. Peter Sedgwick for initially appointing me to the staff of St. Michael's College in Cardiff, Wales. My experience as a Dean of Residential Training and then as Acting Principal suggested to me that a book like this is much needed, especially for those anticipating active ministry in the church today. Such men and women face a daunting task; I believe there are too few trying to inspire them to meet their future responsibilities with joy and hope. I am also enormously grateful to the Right Rev. Wyn Evans and to the Ven. Dennis Wight for inviting me in 2014 to lead the ordination retreat at St. Non's Retreat Centre and to preach at the glorious St. David's Cathedral. As I've already said, the retreat gave me the opportunity to reflect deeply on how my academic research might connect with my pastoral experience. One can think of few places better suited to such theological reflection than the magnificent seaside cliffs of Pembrokeshire in late June.

St. Michael's Theological College

Llandaff

— 1 —

Your Ministry and the Gift of Creation

FIFTEEN HUNDRED YEARS AGO when the young Welsh woman Non gave birth to her remarkable son Dewi, or David, she could have had little notion of what he would go on to achieve. Given the fact that Wales was being raided regularly by the rapacious Irish on one side and the even more rapacious English on the other, life for the British in Wales wasn't easy. Life was generally very nasty, very short, and exceptionally brutish. There wasn't much to fill one with hope and even less with happiness. That's why if you read a lot of the literature from that age, you'll find it wasn't exactly optimistic. The general sentiment is evoked by the Anglo-Saxon poem "Wanderer":

> All the kingdom of earth is full of hardship,
> The voice of fate changes the world under heaven.
> Here wealth is lent; here a friend is lent;
> Here a man is lent; here a kinsman is lent,
> The whole foundation of earth becomes empty![1]

Not what you would call cheerful stuff. And the situation was probably worse in St. David's native land in west Wales, a place hardly touched by the benefits of the Roman Empire but enduring all the hard consequences that followed the retreat of the last legions from Britannia. The few Christians then dwelling among wooded hills or along the sheltered coves of Wales must have despaired about the future of their church even more than their distant descendants do today. And yet somehow saints like David

1. Anonymous, "Wanderer," my translation.

still mustered enough zeal for the gospel not only to ensure the survival of Christianity in Wales but also to inspire a host of other saints for future generations to admire (albeit with the help of some later editors) and whose names are now commemorated in towns and villages throughout the land.

Now, one shouldn't romanticize the so-called Celtic saints. Were we to travel in time, I suspect we'd find them unappealing, puritanical, and much of their ministry in poor taste. For all their supposed love for creation and for composing delightful poetry, they also could enforce penitentials few of us would ever care to adopt. The next time you feel tempted to complain about senior clergy, stop for a moment and give thanks that they don't insist on penance should you accidentally break wind during worship. The little that we do know about the British and Irish saints suggests that they were often hard and austere, which isn't surprising given the grim world in which they lived.

At the same time, these early saints shared with Christians of their era a remarkable grasp of the place of God's creation in the outworking of redemption. The world might be brutal and full of darkness, but for them it remained in some mysterious way the garden where the Lord enjoys strolling "at the time of the evening breeze" (Gen 3:8). In his great work on the Trinity, Augustine of Hippo speaks of the "footprints" of God in creation that point us towards God if only we have the eyes to see them.[2] The Psalms reminded them, too, that even the hills dance for joy and all living creatures praise their Creator. Similarly, for example, the sixth-century hymn-writer Venantius Fortunatus sang of creation itself responding to and celebrating Easter:

> Lo, the fair beauty of the earth, from the death of the
>   winter arising,
>
> Every good gift of the year, now with its Master returns.
>
> Daily the loveliness grows, adorned with the glory of
>   blossom;

---

2. Augustine, *On the Trinity* 6.12.

Green is the woodland with leaves, bright are the mead-
ows with flowers.

He who was nailed to the cross is Lord and the ruler of
all things;

All things created on earth worship the Maker of all.[3]

This is just one of many examples where creation is portrayed as participating in the fruits of redemption rather than standing apart from them. It's a vision that one rarely encounters today.

Instead, we have reduced the scope of our faith to the individual: more often than not an aspect of a person's lifestyle. We're much more comfortable with speaking about what God means to us than about how the whole cosmos relates to him. "Me and God" nudges out not only our neighbors but also creation—in the process we lose our sense of relation to each other and to the created world in which we live and belong. Consequently, our understanding of what it means to be redeemed also becomes impoverished and idiosyncratic. We define for ourselves what salvation means and mainly turn it into little more than confidence that we'll get into heaven.

But, whereas the church of the past three or four hundred years has tended to play down the role of creation within the great story of salvation, Christians such as St. David saw it as a place filled with the wonder and terror of God, a place of beauty and surprising glimpses of God's glory, and as a place of communion. That's one of the remarkable qualities of their thought; for them the heavenly hosts lurked everywhere (as did, incidentally, those of hell) ready to surprise the unwary with glimpses of divine glory. In this way, creation itself was a sermon, waiting to teach the wise about God. For example, the thirteenth-century Franciscan Bonaventure begins his *Journey of the Mind to God* by declaring:

Whoever, therefore, is not enlightened by such splendor
of created things is blind; whoever is not awakened by
such outcries is deaf; whoever does not discover the First
Principle from such clear signs is a fool. Therefore, open

3. Fortunatus, "Salve, festa dies."

your eyes, alert the ears of your spirit, open your lips
and apply your heart so that in all creatures you may see,
hear, praise, love and worship, glorify and honor your
God lest the whole world rise against you.[4]

And what revealed God perhaps best of all was the beauty of creation in which we delight. Indeed, for them the coinage of this
earthly theater of God's glory is delight. Beneath all their gloomy
language about sin lay the deeper conviction that God actually delights in his creation and that we and all creation have been made
to delight in him. And the reason why they believed this, despite
the hardship of their often short lives, was that Scripture had taught
them that the world is good. Before all else in Scripture stands the
first statement about God: "And God saw that it was good."

That's where I'd like to begin: the goodness of creation. I don't
think we ponder that idea often enough. To state that the material universe is fundamentally good was actually one of the most
shocking claims that the first Christians made. Jews and Greeks
could accept much that Christians believed about God: the idea
that he is transcendent, all-powerful, and all-knowing didn't cause
them any difficulties. That was their conception of the divine, of
the One from which all things flow. But most "educated" people in
the ancient world thought that the physical world was either evil
or a distraction—for them anything that appeals to the five senses
diverts our attention from the real, celestial world that hovers
above us beyond the orbit of the moon. When Christians and Jews
claimed that God freely and generously created everything—both
physical and spiritual—out of nothing, and that this meant everything is inherently good, people thought they were mad. It's why
they also thought Christians were eccentric for maintaining that
Christ rose physically from the dead and that the faithful would be
raised physically at the second coming. Who would want to return
to the prison of their physical bodies? The only concept like salvation that the ancients had was that of being freed from the body so
their purified souls could return to their original place among the
celestial stars. To facilitate that return to the divine was the goal of

4. Bonaventure, "The Soul's Journey into God" 1.15.

4

much of their philosophy. To claim as the earliest Christians did that our physical bodies will enjoy eternity struck many Greeks and Romans as ridiculous; for them it was more than a stumbling block to belief—it was utter foolishness.

So, it's well to remember that the creeds begin with the bold claim that God is the creator of heaven and earth and of all things seen and unseen. No aspect of creation was an accident or a kind of waste product that God never intended to exist. That's what many of the Greeks believed. It was, if you will, the accepted wisdom of the ancient world. And it was a belief against which Christians took a firm stance. Indeed, some of the fiercest battles of the earliest church were over whether the material world, including our bodies, is good and redeemable. All the cultural and philosophical biases of the age pushed Christians the other way, and yet they ultimately stood firm and retained the belief in the goodness of the entire cosmos as central to their understanding of both creation and redemption. Don't overlook the fact that in defending the humanity of Christ against the Gnostics, the church fathers were also defending the goodness of the physical world. We too easily miss the radicalism of the first line of the creed.

The belief that creation is inherently good also committed the first Christians to the idea that human sin couldn't be without consequence to the rest of creation. They thought that the depravity of humankind entailed the corruption of nature too. When humankind fell, they took creation with them. Now, you might think this an absurd idea, especially given what we now know about the size of the cosmos relative to us. How could our fall affect stars and galaxies millions of light years away? I don't think there is a ready answer to that question, though I'll look at the importance of the fall in more detail later. But it is worth noting that the idea that human activity impacts the rest of creation provided an antecedent to our own ecological concerns today; we can now see how our socioeconomic depredations are destroying the planet. In other words, we can see all around us that human morals and values have an enormous impact on the natural world. That we lost sight not only of humanity's place within creation but also creation's place in the eyes of God are key reasons why we find ourselves in such a colossal environmental mess. Detach humanity from the world and we quickly treat that world in the same way we usually do the defenseless: we abuse, oppress, and exploit it. At the root of pollution, toxic landscapes, and global warming lies the mistaken belief that redemption has little or nothing to do with the rest of the world.

But the idea that creation itself is good and loved by God means that creation can never be secondary, as though it were only a stage on which humankind enacts its story. At the heart of the Christian faith is the conviction that our redemption includes the redemption of creation. To say otherwise is to claim either that God brought into existence and sustained creation for no particular reason since it will all be destroyed in the end or that his plans were forever spoiled by our fall when everything came into bondage to corruption and decay. In other words, if creation isn't included in redemption then the central problem of the first part of Genesis—the loss of the happy harmony between God, humankind, and creation (symbolized by Eden)—is never resolved. If creation doesn't at least regain its freedom from corruption then sin wins no matter how many fortunate men and women find eternal bliss in heaven. To understand that better, though, we need first to return to Eden.

The Bible begins with Eden for a reason; the garden is more than a backdrop. Adam and Eve awaken there and there they first encounter God, each other, and all the animals they name. Eden is a garden where everything flourishes. In the ancient world, gardens symbolized fruitfulness, goodness, peace, and good order. Adam and Eve's initial and primary purpose is also related to the garden; they are given the job of tending it. The reference to their "tilling and keeping" (Gen 2:15) the garden is the same phrase that is used elsewhere in the Old Testament to describe the priests "tending and guarding" the temple.[5] Eden is the holy sanctuary of creation and Adam and Eve are its priests. They are created to be God's priestly stewards, to share in his generous love for creation.

5. Beale, "Eden," 7–8.

That image of Adam and Eve, bearers of God's image, naming the animals and living in harmony with both the plants and animals of the earth and with God is the Genesis ideal that re-echoes through the pages of Scripture.

So, according to 1 Kings 6, the walls and columns of the holy of holies in the temple in Jerusalem were decorated with carvings of palm trees, pomegranates, and open flowers. These were the symbols of Eden and reminded the Jews of God's continued presence in the world. The lamp stand outside the entrance was decorated to look like a tree, symbolizing perhaps the tree of life in the garden. Ezekiel later fills his vision of a restored Israel with images of Eden as does Psalm 36:8–9: "They feast on the abundance of your house, and you give them drink from the river of your delights [*literally* your Edens]. For with you is the fountain of life, and in your light we shall see light." And famously Isaiah prophesizes:

> The wilderness and the dry land shall be glad;
>
> the desert shall rejoice and blossom;
>
> like the crocus it shall blossom abundantly,
>
> and rejoice with joy and singing . . .
>
> They shall see the glory of the Lord,
>
> the majesty of our God . . .
>
> Say to those who are of a fearful heart,
>
> "Be strong, do not fear!
>
> Here is your God.
>
> He will come with vengeance,
>
> with terrible recompense.
>
> He will come and save you.
>
> Then the eyes of the blind shall be opened,
>
> and the ears of the deaf unstopped;
>
> then the lame shall leap like a deer,
>
> and the tongue of the speechless sing for joy.
>
> For waters shall break forth in the wilderness,

and streams in the desert;

the burning sand shall become a pool,

and the thirsty ground springs of water . . .

And the ransomed of the Lord shall return

and come to Zion with singing;

everlasting joy shall be upon their heads;

they shall obtain joy and gladness,

and sorrow and sighing shall flee away." (Isa 35:1–10)

Throughout the Old Testament, the image of Eden intertwines with the image of the temple, and in the hands of the prophets becomes the symbolic landscape of the new and restored Israel.[6]

The Genesis ideal appears again at the fulcrum moment of history: the resurrection. Where in Genesis we have the six days of creation followed by God's Sabbath rest before the scene opens in the garden of Eden with Adam, in John's gospel we have the six days of Holy Week followed by Jesus' Sabbath rest in the tomb before the scene opens on Easter morning in the garden with Jesus.[7] This aspect of Holy Saturday is commemorated in the Orthodox liturgy, which proclaims, "This is the most blessed Sabbath on which Christ sleeps, but on the third day he shall rise again."[8] And just in case you miss the parallel, John makes sure to include in his narrative the story of Mary Magdalene initially mistaking Jesus for being a gardener. Really it was no mistake at all: Jesus is the gardener of the new creation. Or in the words of St. Paul, he is the new Adam (1 Cor 15:45). Writing in the early seventeenth century, the great Anglican bishop Lancelot Andrewes (responsible for the translation of the Pentateuch for the Authorized Version of the Bible) had this to say about the scene: Mary Magdalene, he wrote,

> did not mistake in taking Him for a gardener. . . . For in
> a sense, and a good sense, Christ may well be said to be

6. Ibid., 5–7.

7. See Wright, *The Challenge of Jesus,* 174–76, for an excellent discussion of this point.

8. Hopko, *Orthodox Faith.*

a gardener, and indeed is one. For our rule is, Christ as He appears, so He is ever; no false semblant in Him. 1. A gardener He is then. The first, the fairest garden that ever was, Paradise. He was the gardener, it was of His planting. So, a gardener. 2. And ever since it is He that as God makes all our gardens green, sends us yearly the spring, and all the herbs and flowers we then gather; and neither Paul with his planting, nor Apollos with his watering, could do any good without Him. So a gardener in that sense. 3. But not in that alone; but He it is who gardens our "souls" too, and makes them . . . "like a well-watered garden"; weeds out of them whatsoever is noisome or unsavoury, sows and plants them with true roots and seeds of righteousness, waters them with the dew of His grace, and makes them bring forth fruit to eternal life. But it is none of all these, but besides all these, no over and above all these, this day if ever, most properly He was a gardener . . . Christ rising was indeed a gardener, and that a strange one, Who made such a herb grow out of the ground this day as the like was never seen before, a dead body to shoot forth alive out of the grave.[9]

What better sign of the new creation than the appearance of Jesus in the garden? Here we find not only the new Adam in the new garden but also (if you keep in mind the biblical echoes) the presence of God in his holy of holies. That Easter scene speaks of new beginnings.

And then Eden appears one final time at the end of that strange book, the Revelation of St. John, which we modern-day Christians often find more than a little off-putting. Its vision of "a new heaven and the new earth" is of Eden restored with the temple thrown in. From the heavenly Jerusalem, in which the temple "is the Lord God Almighty and the Lamb," flows the river of life from city as it had from Eden and is sheltered under the shadow of the tree of life, the leaves of which are for the healing of the nations (Rev 21–22). The images of Eden, the temple, and the new creation all merge in John's vision of the new Jerusalem—the fulfilled kingdom of God that embraces both heaven and earth.

9. Andrewes, "Sermon XIV," 15–16.

If we have at the beginning of the Bible an image of perfect creation, we find it again at the crucial moment of Christ's resurrection, and conclude with it in the final two chapters of the New Testament. That image pervades Scripture and so draws us back, if we have the poetic sensibilities to appreciate it, again and again to that image of God delighting and wanting to delight in his creation. That image provides, if you will, the backdrop for understanding our own redemption—it is the context for our own creation, lies at the heart of God's glory dwelling in the temple, situates the Easter story of our redemption, and beckons us to plunge more deeply into the new creation of God's kingdom. Creation is God's greatest gift to us—a gift he freely and generously gave and continues to give, a gift he will never cast aside let alone consume with fire. Creation was formed with us, redeemed with us, and it will be transformed with us.

Reflect on that idea for a moment. So much of Christianity today and for the last 200 years has been presented as an almost entirely private affair that is mainly about doing what's necessary to escape this world and get past St. Peter the heavenly bouncer through the pearly gates. Christianity has been reduced to a mercenary religion in which the only worthwhile question seems to be, "What must I do to inherit eternal life?" And that really means "what is the *minimum* I must do to make it into heaven?" Moreover, we've lost sight of the idea that our own bodies will share in our resurrection, often promoting instead the belief that the afterlife involves our spirits escaping our bodies to dwell in an ethereal heaven. Within such a bland vision of the Christian faith, doing good, being stewards of the earth, and building up communities became secondary, either things we ought to do to show that we've been saved or a rationale for our being useful to our society while we're on the way to heaven. That's also why when modern Christians worried about social injustices, they didn't immediately see what role faith had to play and so often made that faith secondary to the task of doing justice. Broadly speaking, we have there the divide between conservative and liberal Christians. But the Bible sees both ideas as inextricably intertwined. The whole reason why

God bothers to "save" us is not so he can enjoy our charming company in heaven but so we can return to the reason why he created us in the first place: to be stewards of his creation and to share with creation in his delight.

It's that idea—that God saves us *for* his creation—that needs to be at the heart of our ministries, be we clergy or laity. The mission of the church isn't to random people in our world but to our world through the people we bring into God's kingdom. The mission of the church isn't separate and compartmentalized from the world in which it's conducted; it includes that world every bit as much as it includes the people of that world. That's why the church's mission is always a public one. In that sense, our ministry is less like a rescue mission than a reclamation project—the rescuing has already been accomplished by Christ.

But what exactly does it mean to be saved by God *for* his creation? In one of his most insightful essays, Rowan Williams explains it in this way:

> Humanity, in the Genesis story, names the animals; the calling of the human person is to name the world aright, that is, to acknowledge it as God's gift and to work so as to bring to light its character as reflecting God's character, to manifest its true essence. Thus it is common to describe the vocation of human beings in this context as "liturgical": human beings orchestrate the reflection of God's glory in the world by clothing material things with sacred meaning and presenting the world before God in prayer. Worship is not only a matter of words, but is a foretaste of the God-related destiny of the world, that longed-for state of creation in which everything can be clearly seen as bearing God's glory and love. And one signal and important aspect of sin is the refusal of human beings to undertake this calling, to refuse to act in a "priestly" way towards the environment—to refuse to bless and give thanks, to refuse the right use of material things.[10]

That's our shared calling: to bless and give thanks for creation, to function as the mouthpiece of all God's creatures by raising their

10. Williams, "Changing the Myths We Live By," 178.

praises to the Father from whom all blessings flow. That's what it means to be stewards of God's delight. This vision of the Christian faith has its feet as firmly planted on the earth as its head is stuck in the heavens. It's not detached from the concerns (human and ecological) of the world nor does it fall short of a heavenly perspective. Rather, like a good priest or a temple, it brings both together and thereby lays hold of the sacramental character of creation; only sin makes God and his creation seem estranged from one another. In that respect, our mission is nuptial: we say to a world that tries to hold heaven and earth apart that they are actually united—"what God has brought together let no one set asunder" speaks not only to marriage but to the whole mission of God to the world.

This vision might strike you as novel. Isn't the whole point of our faith to get into heaven? That's certainly what a lot of hymns and funeral sermons would lead you to believe. But this sacramental view of our existence and purpose isn't new—just often forgotten. You can see this older understanding, for example, in a seventeenth-century poem by George Herbert:

> Beasts fain would sing; birds ditty to their notes;
> Tree would be tuning on their native lute
> To thy renown: but all their hands and throats
> Are brought to Man, while they are lame and mute.
>
> Man is the world's high Priest: he doth present
> The sacrifice for all; while they below
> Unto the service mutter an assent,
> Such as springs use that fall, and winds that blow.[11]

To see ourselves as God's royal priesthood set within the midst of God's creation is to begin to take seriously our duty not just to God and to each other but also to his creation. In that sense, the world is our parish and all her creatures our congregation.

Just think how differently we would perceive both worship and our place in the natural world if we thought of attending church in terms of offering to God the praise of all living creatures. When we say our prayers, sing hymns, and participate in

---

11. Herbert, "Providence," ll.31–34. Modernization by me.

the Eucharist together we do so not for our own selfish needs or desires but on behalf of all those creatures—mineral, vegetable, and animal—that are "lame and mute" when it comes to singing to God's "renown." Perhaps like the holy of holies in the temple, we should decorate our churches with natural motifs to remind us that we worship God on behalf of all created things. Ultimately, that is what it means to be God's priesthood.

But this image of humanity as a priesthood really only works if we think of creation as a community. It's not so much that the rest of creation can't share in the praise of God without us as it is that the community of creation *as a whole* doesn't praise God properly unless we fulfill our role as creation's priesthood. I believe this is the reason that Paul can suggest that all of creation longs for us to be redeemed. Through our redemption, the community of creation can regain its freedom from the corruption and decay in which we are implicated. In Romans 8:19–24a, he declares:

> For the creation waits with eager longing for the revealing of the children of God; for the creation was subjected to futility, not of its own will but by the will of the one who subjected it, in hope that the creation itself will be set free from its bondage to decay and obtain the freedom of the glory of the children of God. We know that the whole creation has been groaning together in labor pains until now; and not only the creation, but we ourselves, who have the first fruits of the Spirit, groan inwardly while we wait for adoption, the redemption of our bodies. For in hope we were saved.

In other words, the community of all created things awaits our becoming proper priests again so that its relationship with God can be repaired. The wild and tangled garden of the earth is yearning for us to return to being priestly gardeners so that it can again break forth with the flowers of paradise.

And this is precisely the message (as we'll see in more depth later) we are meant to hear when we read the various accounts of the resurrection: all those uncanny stories about Jesus appearing and reappearing and passing through locked doors and yet capable of eating fish and being touched by Mary Magdalene and Thomas. In his delightful book, *Miracles*, C. S. Lewis writes:

> [The resurrection] is not a picture of an escape from any and every kind of Nature into some unconditioned and utterly transcendent life. It is the picture of a new human nature, and a new Nature in general, being brought into existence. We must, indeed, believe the risen body to be extremely different from the mortal body: but the existence, in that new state, of anything that could in any sense be described as "body" at all, involves some sort of spatial relations and in the long run a whole new universe. That is the picture—not of unmaking but of remaking. The old field of space, time, matter, and the senses is to be weeded, dug, and sown for a new crop. We may be tired of that field: God is not.[12]

And this new life, says so much of Scripture, is what it truly means to be alive—to enjoy existence free from the corrosion of sin and death. This is the abundant life that Christ promises us. This is what we offer to others. This is what it means to be stewards of delight and priests of the new creation.

To be priests of the new creation is a vocation to which all Christians are called. Now, that may be news to you. We live in a church of leadership initiatives and managerial philosophies. We live in a church that too easily gets distracted by the need to register baptisms, weddings, and funerals, account for money, assess performance, worry about closures and regulations, and all the necessary but often soul-sucking needs of a bureaucratic institution embedded within a world of policies, regulations, and legal frameworks. Certainly, much of that is necessary just as budgeting, keeping track of receipts, getting insurance, and the like are essential chores for a healthy family life. But too often we become so focused on such things that we forget what the ministry—what the church—is truly about, which is proclaiming, anticipating and enacting the new creation. How much more appealing would our ministries be if they were shaped by a vision of the new creation

---

12. Lewis, *Miracles*, 178.

that sought to make Eden, the temple, the resurrection, and the heavenly Jerusalem sensible to our contemporary world?

That we are the priesthood of the new creation is why the church is supposed to be subversive. At the heart of the gospel is God's judgment on every aspect of our lives and on a human society that so often diminishes life and obstructs love. It's also why people should encounter something so astonishingly differ- ent when they experience a Christian community that they come away, like the Thessalonians in Acts, claiming that we are turning the world upside-down (Acts 17:6). That we've largely lost the ca- pacity to be windows through which people may glimpse the new creation is no small reason why churches so often fail to inspire.

What does that new life in the new creation look like? In the following chapters of this little book, I'll try to answer that ques- tion by focusing on the generosity of the Trinity, God's renewal of creation, his immeasurable delight, and finally the divine love that underpins and enfolds all. It seems to me that unless we begin to see how our ministries can participate in the renewal of creation through the free generosity of God's delightful love, we'll continue to fall short of our calling. I hope the vision I present will inspire you, give you a sense of purpose, and help you to become an as- tonishing member of the church, the body of Christ. Most of all, however, I hope this vision will give you a glimpse of the mag- nificent tapestry of God's creative and redemptive love for all of creation. For only by glimpsing God's unfathomable love for his whole creation can we truly become the priesthood of all believers he has called us to be. Only by allowing the Genesis ideal to be- come our own ideal can we be stewards of God's delight by offering the gospel of God's love to a world filled with despair.

2

Your Ministry and the Generosity of the Trinity

I'M GOING TO START this chapter by saying something you may find shocking: God doesn't need you. I'm sorry if people have said that he does when they suggested you think about the ministry. But it simply isn't true. God doesn't need you. He doesn't need me. He doesn't need any of us or the whole cosmos in the slightest for that matter. Were we all to vanish, God would remain every bit the same God he is now and always has been. God doesn't need us for anything.

The fact that God doesn't need you or me is one of the main things we mean when we speak of God as being totally free. He never acts under necessity and is never compelled to do anything. For example, he didn't need creation in order to have something or someone to love; Father, Son and Holy Spirit share each other's love eternally and, indeed, are love. God is infinite and supreme freedom itself, which, needless to say, is impossible for us to imagine. I suspect if we try, we invariably imagine chaos: God the cosmic toddler.

So God is free. God doesn't need anything, including you and me. "To have free choice befits God" is how Thomas Aquinas put it in an understated fashion.[1] Although this is a bedrock Christian belief, it's apparently news to a lot of people. I performed an online search for the phrase "God needs" and these are some of the hits it produced:

1. Aquinas, *Summa contra Gentiles* 1.88

"God needs you"

"God needs men/women today"

"God needs workers in his vineyard"

"God needs our prayers"

"God needs more enemies" (I'm sure he's grateful for that piece of advice)

"God needs an army to save America" (my personal favorite)

"God needs witnesses"

"God needs the Church to do his will"

. . . and so on. Now, to be fair a lot of these are trying to get an important message across—namely, that Christians need to get off their backsides—but they all get the need backwards. God doesn't actually need us to do anything, which admittedly might explain the lifestyle of some clergy.

Well, this is all very cheery isn't it? Most of us don't like being reminded that we're extraneous and unneeded. Quite the opposite: the desire to be needed is arguably one of the most fundamental of human desires. So why on earth have I begun a chapter on God's generosity by reminding you that God doesn't need you? There are several reasons why I think it's important to start this way.

First, most people who sense God calling them to ministry need their egos pricked at least a little. Believing that we're called to be a Christian minister can be a heady experience. It's easy to become convinced that God is actually speaking to us in a special way; this conviction can then quickly turn into the conclusion that we must therefore be special. This danger is especially acute for those who sense a vocation to the ordained ministry. As with weddings, ordinations are occasions when everyone goes out of their way to make those on center stage feel special—frankly, an odd impulse given that those on center stage normally feel special already. Those about to be ordained end up with a stack of sentimental ordination cards that make all sorts of extraordinary claims about them. What a wonderful privilege God has called them to enjoy! What amazing people they are for dedicating their lives to the service of others! Isn't it marvelous that God has chosen them to be priests or deacons? All nonsense. As John the Baptist reminded the Pharisees, God can raise followers from rocks if he wants to—and they'd probably be a lot more enterprising too. So, don't allow the admiration of others to fool you into thinking you're somebody special. Plumbers typically provide more benefit to others in the course of their day than we clergy do.

Second, if we say that God needs us to do this, that, or the other, then we're really saying that God Almighty in some way depends on us. We like that idea, don't we? It makes us feel important. Notice how often Christian rhetoric can portray God as a kind of cosmic damsel in distress and the faithful (however you want to define them) as his brave knights in shining armor. I can't count how many Christians I've known who have defined their ministry in terms of protecting God from his purported enemies: dangerous liberals, narrow-minded conservatives, naive evangelicals, or idolatrous Catholics. But to say that God doesn't need us, that he doesn't depend on us, means that he also doesn't need our protection or even our support. He's perfectly capable of taking care of himself. In fact, God is so free from depending on us that no matter what we do, we'll further his plans. C. S. Lewis puts this point memorably in the *Problem of Pain*:

> A merciful man aims at his neighbor's good and so does "God's will," consciously co-operating with "the simple good." A cruel man oppresses his neighbor, and so does simple evil. But in doing such evil, he is used by God, without his own knowledge or consent, to produce the complex good—so that the first man serves God as a son, and the second as a tool. For you certainly carry out God's purposes, however you act, but it makes a difference to you whether you serve like Judas or like John.[2]

In that sense, not only can we not put God in our debt but we also can never escape his own absolute freedom; his freedom surrounds us and overwhelms our own pretense at freedom so that no

2. Lewis, *The Problem of Pain*, 89.

matter what we do, God remains absolutely free from us and our attempts to cage him. We do well to remember that.

But the main reason I've begun this way is that it helps to remind us that if God doesn't need anything, then he always acts out of complete freedom and generosity. He does whatever he does because he wills to do it, not because he's obliged. God's only motive is love. Everything God does, therefore, is entirely a gift. God didn't need to create, he generously chose to do so; God didn't need to call Abraham, he generously chose to do so; he didn't need to rescue the Hebrews from bondage, he generously chose to do so; he didn't need to redeem us by the cross, he generously chose to do so; he doesn't need to remake the world, he generously chooses to do so; God doesn't need you to minister to others; he generously chooses you to share in that privilege. God is generous because God is absolute freedom.

The generous freedom of God and particularly what that might say about us as created human beings are ideas that have fascinated the brightest minds of the church. For example, the belief that God freely chose to create and sustain both the physical and spiritual world intrigued medieval theologians, many of whom had rejected that world by becoming monks. Aelred of Reivaulx declared in a Pentecost sermon, "from the beginning, the Spirit of the Lord has filled the whole world, uniting all, sustaining all, ordering and arranging all. . . . Since all creatures made from nothing were naturally unstable and perishable, arising and disappearing, and tending towards oblivion, the goodness of God alone, which is his Spirit, joined and guided them, and lent them his own immutable stability . . . ."[3] So, creation isn't accidental but an intentional act of love by God. In his *Summa contra Gentiles*, Aquinas echoed this idea by methodically arguing "that God acts, in the realm of created things, not by necessity of His nature, but by the free choice of His will."[4] His contemporary, the Franciscan Bonaventure, turned to the mystical writings of Pseudo-Dionysius to argue that creation arises from the "self-diffusive" and fecund

3. Quoted in Sommerfeldt, *Aelred of Reivaulx*, 2.
4. Aquinas, *Summa contra Gentiles* 2.23

nature of God, so that everything that exits somehow partakes of God's infinite and unstinting generosity.[5] In other words, we not only thank God for freely creating and sustaining us, but in some mysterious way we also partake of and share in that generosity. In more recent times, the great German theologian Jürgen Moltmann has echoed this medieval approach by linking God's freedom with his love:

> When we say that God created the world "out of freedom,"
> we must immediately add "out of love." God's freedom is
> not the almighty power for which everything is possible.
> It is love, which means the self-communication of the
> good. If God creates the world out of freedom, then he
> creates it out of love. . . . In doing this he is entirely free,
> and in this freedom he is entirely himself.[6]

What sort of God is this who freely and generously chooses to create and to love his creation? Certainly, he is unlike anything we encounter in this world.

Think about your experience of love for a moment. Can you imagine a love that is totally free, that is so completely self-giving that it makes no space for need? Perhaps on some sentimental level you can, but I suspect you probably can't picture a realistic love in that way. If your dearest companion said to you, "I love you but I don't really need you," you'd be insulted. We want the people we love to need us, though perhaps not too much. Our very first experience of love as children is very much need-love. We depend on our parents to show us affection and to meet our needs; even before we're conscious of ourselves the fact that they meet our physical and emotional needs (or fail to do so) becomes the foundation for our whole concept of love. Let's face it, generally speaking if we don't need something, we ignore it, cast it aside, or abuse it; we rarely love it.

If this is true, then to say that God is totally free and that he loves us presents us with a quandary. How can he both love and not need us? I suppose we get a hint of what an answer might look like

5. Bonaventure, "The Soul's Journey into God" 6.1.

6. Moltmann, *God in Creation*, 75–76.

when we become parents. We love our children but we don't need them to love us—actually, at first we just need them to let us sleep for more than three hours straight during the night. Certainly, we'd feel acutely the loss of their love if they stopped loving us or died, but we don't depend on their love in the same way they depend on ours. In fact, needy parents can do great psychological harm to their children. So, parenthood gives us a glimpse of the kind of love God provides us. But it's only a vague shadow of his love.

Part of the reason why we find God's sort of love difficult to grasp is that we don't really understand what it means to be truly generous. Our generosity normally springs from material excess. We speak of wealthy benefactors as being generous when they donate a fraction of their disposable income to a worthy cause. We think of ourselves as generous when we drop a few coins in a charity box. We're on slightly better ground when we call a friend generous who derives pleasure from wining and dining his or her friends with no expectation of recompense. And perhaps we're on equally good ground when we refer to someone who is liberal-minded and accepting of other people's views as being generous in mind. But again these are only vague shadows of a truly fulsome generosity.

At the heart of both generosity and freedom is the idea of selflessness, of being so self-giving that the self vanishes. And this true generosity is one of the prime attributes of the God we worship. Bonaventure described God as the "fountain fullness" of goodness. By this he meant that God holds nothing back. "It is the nature of God," writes the Franciscan scholar Ilia Delio while describing Bonaventure's views, "to give Godself away in love."[7] That complete and total pouring out of oneself into the other lies at the heart of the Trinity:

> For good is said to be self-diffusive. But the greatest self-diffusion cannot exist unless it is actual and intrinsic, substantial and hypostatic, natural and voluntary, free and necessary, lacking nothing and perfect. Therefore, unless there were eternally in the highest good a production which is actual and consubstantial, and a hypostasis

7. Delio, *Simply Bonaventure*, 50.

as noble as the producer, as in the case in producing by way of generation and spiration, so that it is from an eternal principle eternally coproducing, so that there would be beloved and a cobeloved, the one generated and the other spirated, and this is the Father and the Son and the Holy Spirit—unless there were present, it would by no means be the highest good because it would not diffuse itself in the highest degree.[8]

In other words, for God to be perfect he must be eternally self-communicating goodness, giving himself entirely to the other; for Bonaventure, this requires a God who can share in that self-emptying as beloved and co-beloved. Because of this, he could claim that, like his hero St. Francis, the Father is actually poor—indeed, supremely so—because he generously gives to the Son all that he is and all that he has. For Bonaventure, generous self-emptying lies at the very heart of the Trinity.

And it's out of this inexhaustible generosity that God creates and sustains the world. According to Hans Boersma,

> For Christians, the Creation was not an automatic or necessary emanation flowing from the being of God without an intervening act of his will. Creation was not simply an excretion from preexisting matter or spirit. Rather, God created the world freely—*ex nihilo* (out of nothing). While creating the world was certainly a fitting or congruous thing for God to do, it was not a necessary act. Creation did not simply emanate from the being of God.[9]

So, the idea that God freely created the world out of nothing shows that God's generosity in creating is thorough and complete; there isn't an atom in the universe that he either *had* to create or that exists without God having called it into existence. Bonaventure refers to creation as a mere point, a speck, in the generous love shared by the Father, Son, and Holy Spirit.[10] We and the whole universe are, therefore, produced and swept up by God's eternal generosity.

8. Bonaventure, "The Soul's Journey into God" 6.2
9. Boersma, *Heavenly Participation*, 33–34.
10. Bonaventure, "The Soul's Journey into God" 6.2.

Everything we know, everything we perceive, and everything we are exists because of God's outflowing love: "In him was life, and the life was the light of all people" (John 1:4). In his delightful little book, *Tokens of Trust*, Rowan Williams writes, "God is to be trusted as we would trust a loving parent, whose commitment to us is inexhaustible, whose purposes for us are unfailingly generous; someone whose life is the source of our life, and who guarantees that there is always a home for us."[11] Divine generosity is the wellspring of created existence, woven as it were into the fiber of our being. To be generous, therefore, is more than a virtuous act; it is to act according to the blueprint of our own being.

God's freedom and generosity are also demonstrated in our redemption. Christ did not need to become one of us and certainly did not need to die for our salvation. He chose to do both out of that same free generosity that expresses his relationship to the Father and the Holy Spirit. "But God proves his love for us in that while we still were sinners," declares Paul, "Christ died for us" (Rom 5:8). Christ's death on the cross is the ultimate sign of God's generous love towards humankind. It reveals the shape of that divine generosity by demonstrating God's love in the midst of human cruelty; it plumbs the depths of that love, too, by showing us in this life the extent of God's self-diffusive goodness: "Let the same mind be in you that was in Christ Jesus, who, though he was in the form of God, did not regard equality with God as something to be exploited, but emptied himself, taking the form of a slave, being born in human likeness. And being found in human form, he humbled himself and became obedient to the point of death—even death on a cross" (Phil 2:5–8).

And through the cross and the empty tomb we receive by faith the gift of the Holy Spirit. The image of God's Spirit as a gift is one of the most common metaphors in the New Testament for the Holy Spirit. So, for example, in Acts 2:38, Peter assures the crowds on Pentecost that if they repent and are baptized, they will "receive the gift of the Holy Spirit." Augustine understood the Holy Spirit

11. Williams, *Tokens of Trust*, 90.

as being a gift in two ways. First of all, he is the gift of communion shared by the Father and the Son:

> The Holy Spirit is a kind of inexpressible communion or fellowship of Father and Son, and perhaps he is given this name just because the same name can be applied to the Father and the Son. He is properly called what they are called in common, seeing that both the Father and the Son are holy and both the Father and the Son are spirit. So to signify the communion of them both by a name which applies to them both, the gift of both is called the Holy Spirit.[12]

The Holy Spirit is, therefore, the shared communion, shared love, and shared gift of the Father and the Son. What word expresses that threefold identity better than generosity? Second, the Holy Spirit is the gift given to us. Augustine writes:

> So the love which is from God and is God is distinctively the Holy Spirit; through him the charity of God is poured out into our hearts, and through it the whole triad dwells in us. This is the reason why . . . the Holy Spirit, while being God, should also be called the gift of God. And this gift, surely, is distinctively to be understood as being the charity that brings us through to God, without which no other gift of God at all can bring us through to God.[13]

So, the Holy Spirit, who God pours into our hearts and who is identified as the generous gift of communion shared by the Father and the Son, is also the generous gift that grants us salvation. In God's own generosity we were created and are redeemed.

That God creates and redeems out of his inexhaustible generosity rather than out of need tells us a great deal about ourselves and creation. Generosity and freedom lie at the heart of our existence and of everything around us. God loves so completely that he pours out his generosity and freedom into all that he creates. In terms of the Genesis ideal, it also means that God's generous freedom defines the purpose of our existence—that in some manner

12. Augustine, *On the Trinity* 5.12.

13. Ibid., 15.32.

(that we'll explore later) generosity should be the hallmark of what humanity seeks to do and achieve both in the present and over time. In other words, we are called not only to be the priesthood of the community of creation but also through that priesthood to express God's freedom and generosity. The world is meant to be free; the world is meant to be awash with generosity. As I said in the last chapter, that freedom is the goal of redemption—to be redeemed from corruption, sin, and darkness is nothing more or less than to be brought back into the mainstream of God's freedom and generosity.

And so, in a very real sense, whenever we speak of love, we should have in mind a wildly free generosity that leaves absolutely no space for an independent, autonomous self. "Those who lose their life for my sake will find it" (Matt 10:39) is what Jesus promised. But more importantly, he demonstrated that kind of love by becoming one of us and embracing death upon the cross for our redemption. We see in Christ's life and death the perfect expression within human history of God's "fountain fullness," of God's absolute generosity. It is so overwhelming that it swallows up even death. God holds nothing back but rather pours himself out completely.

This free generosity then underpins a great deal of Christian ethics. How do we as Christian conduct our lives in a way that speaks to God's own inexhaustible generosity? We take to heart that it is more blessed to give than to receive. We love our neighbors as ourselves. We love our enemies. We love without counting the costs. We give up our wealth to follow Christ. Most importantly we love God with all our heart, with all our soul, and with all our strength—in other words, we respond to God's creative generosity with our own meager generosity, returning all that he has given us, including our very being, to him. And it is in this way that we then become "filled up into the fullness of God" (Eph 3:19). The more we pour ourselves out into God and through him to others, the more we are filled with the presence of Christ; only then do we start to become truly ourselves because we begin to share fruitfully in the life of the Trinity.

Now, before I discuss how this connects with your future ministry, I want you first to consider just how different all this is from the society in which we live. We live in the age of mass consumption. Our whole way of life from cradle to grave is based on consuming. Our whole economy preaches, as it were, that it's actually much more blessed to receive than to give. We spend an inordinate amount of our time either shopping or thinking about shopping. We become possessed by the mere need to possess. Moreover, as the Catholic theologian William Cavanaugh has cogently argued, we have become defined by consumption so manic that it can only produce waste:

> Most people are not overly attached to things, and most are not obsessed with hoarding riches . . . . What really characterizes culture is not attachment to things but detachment. People do not hoard money; they spend it. People do not cling to things; they discard them and buy other things.[14]

Detachment and waste represent the very opposite of the goodness that arises from God's generosity and freedom. Unlike God, our world cannot indefinitely satisfy our insatiable hunger, and so instead of tending and keeping creation as God's image-bearing priests, raising its praise and thanksgiving to God, we are instead destroying it through our willful and arrogant domination. Called to be like the elves in *The Lord of the Rings*, we have chosen instead to be like Saruman.

Among other things, this means that our attempts to manifest the free generosity of God are more acutely needed than ever. Part of the mission of the church in a world bent on destroying itself is to exhibit a way of living freely and generously. Part of that mission is also to resist and challenge consumer society and the associated assumption that our personal desires, interests, and identities should take priority. Pursuing the common good and seeking to be free from our own special interests are two powerful social ways that the church can manifest the generosity of the God we worship.

14. Cavanaugh, *Being Consumed,* 34.

There's another more subtle way in which we fail to express God's generosity: our obsession with identity. This presents itself in more ways than can be covered in this little book. Broadly speaking, identity is about finding our place in a confusing world by defining ourselves against others and especially against society. We all want to be individuals, to express ourselves in a way that attracts the attention of others. Our whole idea of lifestyles is predicated on the belief that we can shape and adorn our identity to distinguish ourselves from the many and to associate ourselves with a few. The church, of course, is full of this kind of thinking. Much of it is for good reason, as people try to rebalance power dynamics by sharing power more widely among others and especially the marginalized. But the problem with rebalancing power through identity politics is that it invariably leads to tribalism as each identity group pits itself against the other. How different would the world and the church be if everyone were so generous, so willing to pour themselves out into others, that they lost all notion of self-identity or at least the kind of self-identity that distinguishes itself from other identities and looks primarily to protecting its own interests. That such a notion probably strikes many as impossibly idealistic should give you some idea of how far we all have fallen from the freedom and generosity God offers.

Part of the reason why we think it's an impossible ideal is that we all know that such completely self-giving people are invariably taken for granted and manipulated. And let's face it: since we do precisely the same with God, why should people treat us any differently? One of the hard truths of life is that people take advantage of those who are generous—before you know it, a generous person either becomes an enabler or is left with little else to give. Getting generosity right is one of the hardest jobs Christians have faced; some Romans ridiculed early Christians for their gullibility and the ease with which they were conned by fraudsters.

Unfortunately, there is no easy solution to that problem. Living as we do in a fallen world, generosity will invariably be costly (which, of course, generosity by its very nature is). Seeking to live freely through generous self-giving requires discernment so that the gift of yourself is received for the benefit of others rather than to their detriment. But God does give grace in the giving; if we can't always ensure that our generosity is beneficial, we can be certain that our generosity is always received by God as an acceptable sacrifice. As G. K. Chesterton pointed out, the one thing with which the road to hell is definitely not paved is good intentions! Through generosity we are conformed to the image of Christ.

This means, however, that right from the start you have your work cut out for you as a steward of God's delight. How on earth is anyone supposed to express the free generosity of God within their ministries? How on earth are we to make our churches places of generosity and freedom?

If it makes you feel any better, this is a question that has befuddled Christians from the start. Acts presents us on the one hand with the ideal of Christians initially living together in profound communion with one another: "Day by day, as they spent much time together in the temple, they broke bread at home and ate their food with glad and generous hearts, praising God and having the goodwill of all the people" (Acts 2:46–47). But we're also shown from the start that many fell short of that ideal: the story of Sapphira and Ananias being struck dead for lying about their own possessions is a stark reminder that not all Christians found generosity easy. And the fact that Barnabas was especially commended for donating his property to the church (Acts 4:36–37) implies that it was a noteworthy gesture. Then, in Paul's first letter to the Corinthians we see the struggle to encourage freedom and generosity without yielding to license. "All things are lawful" exclaims Paul, "but not all things are edifying" (1 Cor 10:23). True freedom and true generosity build up and profit others rather than ourselves. How hard it is for us Christians to believe that.

Part of the problem is that we tend to quantify and define freedom selfishly. For us, freedom means freedom *to* or freedom *from*. "I'm free to do what I want" was a popular anthem in the '90s and much of our political debate now focuses on how to ensure that we are free from terror. Generally speaking, we use the word *freedom* to mean having the space or ability to do as we like without fear or outside interference. One of the pillars of Western society is personal freedom—the freedom to choose whatever we like as long as it doesn't visibly harm others (we're less concerned if we can't actually see the effect of our choices on others, as sweat shops and toxic wastelands demonstrate). Moreover, our belief in the "freedom to choose" is itself shaped by consumer society so that we yearn to express our individual freedom by shopping for whatever goods and services we are encouraged to desire. Very often our idea of freedom actually leads to economic, social, and emotional bondage.

Our identity as consumers also affects how we perceive the church. Whereas the old *Book of Common Prayer* speaks of worship as presenting and offering "ourselves, our souls and bodies, to be a reasonable, holy, and living sacrifice,"[15] many people today look to "get something out" of attending church. In the course of your ministry, you'll often hear people saying, "I attended St. Swithun's but the service or the sermon didn't do anything for me." Or if we're slightly higher-minded, we'll say that some form of worship doesn't "nourish" us. In both cases, the worship that is supposed to orient us towards God is instead turned towards us, our needs, and our tastes.

So what are you to do? First, let me say that the very idea of categorizing freedom and generosity is a bit absurd. It's a bit like listing in detail how you think someone might be more themselves! But I think there are few broad ideas I can suggest that you might find helpful.

First, you need to model freedom and generosity in the conduct of your own ministry. This isn't a secondary calling as though we can preach the gospel without it. The gospel faces no more a formidable barrier than an ungenerous spirit or a person in bondage to their own opinions. Indeed, one of the worst plagues God can visit upon a church is the busybody minister with an overdeveloped notion about what it really means to be a Christian. You need to take yourself entirely out of the picture. The ministry isn't about you or your needs. God help your congregation or those to

---

15. *Book of Common Prayer*, 81.

whom you minister if you have even an ounce of the feeling that you *need* something from them. Part of what is supposed to happen at your ordination or commissioning is that you let go of your need for a particular style of ministry. You have been called, like Paul, to be all things to all people. It's precisely in learning through experience and reflection how not to need your people even while you dedicate your life to them that you will grow the most and even begin to model God's own freedom and generosity through the conduct of your ministry.

Second, you need to encourage freedom and generosity among your congregations. They need to know how to love and be loved generously. This will include, of course, encouraging them to give liberally to support the less fortunate—and not just money but also their time and energy. But that only scratches the surface. Encourage your people to welcome others with open arms and to be sufficiently considerate of the needs and joys of their neighbors to respond quickly and meaningfully to them. Also, give Scripture, prayer, worship, fellowship, service, and the sacraments the free space to do the hard work of sanctification; your role is to help facilitate the church's formation of God's people into the generous love of God. Might I also suggest that you make people mindful of congregational cliques, festering personal battles, and destructive grudges? Trickiest of all, you constantly need to encourage your church to be open and generous to the other churches in your community no matter their tradition or political alignments.

Finally, be generous towards your fellow clergy and ministers. One of the things that has struck me powerfully over the years is how often ministers are hypercritical of each other. There's a kind of pervasive collaborative criticism that leads clergy to disparage each other when they put a foot wrong. I can't stress enough how destructive that mind-set is. If you are a clergyperson, try not to allow yourself to be drawn into that dynamic. Rather, edify each other; be eager to build each other up, support each other, carry each other's burdens, and share each other's vision. Be generous to each other so that you together can build up the kingdom of God in your neck of the woods.

Notice that I've repeatedly used the word *need*. I began this chapter by saying that God doesn't need you. Well, it should now be clear that to have any hope of success in your ministry, you very much need God. It's only by receiving God's generous grace, poured out into you through prayer, worship, the sacraments, and the daily rounds of ministering to your people that you will discover the freedom and generosity that are expressions of God himself. That's the God who has called you, the God who leads you, and the God to whom you need to introduce others. For it is only by discovering that eternal freedom and generosity from which all good things flow that your people will discover themselves. Only by being nourished by that eternal freedom and generosity will they become new creations who, whether at work, at play, in conversation, or in their relationships, can be the stewards of delight that God calls all of us to be.

3

Your Ministry and the Renewal of Creation

I WANT FIRST TO take you back to Genesis to look at the story of the fall from a slightly different angle than usual. One of the lessons of the opening chapters of Genesis is that human beings aren't happy with God's generous freedom and that we have a propensity to reject his delight or even to delight in things that aren't fecund, playful, and good. Remember how that story opens with Adam and Eve "tilling and keeping" creation's holy of holies, the garden of Eden, as God's priestly stewards. The Genesis ideal expresses a vision of humanity and creation in complete harmony with God. However one approaches the opening chapters of Genesis, taken on its own terms, it presents us with an enticing vision of how the world and humanity's place within it ought to be. Conversely, Genesis speaks to that persistent niggle we feel that things are at present not as they should be. We read about Eden and reflect upon our own world and we can't help but see a disconnection between the ideal and the reality.

By the time we've read to Genesis 11 we have encountered two worlds: the one of perfection and the other of human wretchedness: "One was made by God, the other by men. That made by God was great and beautiful. Before the Fall it was Adam's joy and the Temple of his Glory. That made by men is a Babel of Confusions; Invented Riches, Pomps and Vanities, brought in by Sin . . ."[1] As we see in Traherne's reflection, Genesis explains the presence of these

---

1. Traherne, *Centuries* 1.7

two worlds through the story of the fall that ushers in the world as we now know and encounter it. Typically, the fall is explained in terms of disobedience: Adam and Eve are told not to eat of the tree of the knowledge of good and evil but they choose to do so and, as a result, suffer the consequences of their disobedience. But notice that more than the serpent's con act is required to convince Eve to eat of the tree; it also takes delight: "So when the woman saw that the tree was good for food, and it was a *delight* to the eyes . . . she took of its fruit and ate" (Gen 3:6). Perhaps the temptation to be like God wouldn't have sufficed to tempt Eve to disobey God. Perhaps she needed to be delighted too.

This is, in fact, the lesson St. Augustine drew from this story. In his commentary on Sermon on the Mount, he uses the story of Eve and the serpent to provide a psychological explanation for temptation and sin:

> For, there are three steps toward the complete commis-
> sion of a sin: suggestion, delight, and consent. The sug-
> gestion is made either through the memory or through
> the bodily sense—when we are seeing or hearing or
> smelling or tasting or touching something. If we delight
> in the enjoyment of this, it must be repressed if the de-
> light is sinful. . . . If consent is given, then a sin is fully
> committed in the heart, and it is known to God . . . .[2]

In the story of Eve and the serpent, we see that delight, which we normally think of in positive terms, can just as easily seduce us to consent to sin. In the story of the fall, we discover that no sooner had we been created to delight in the goodness of God's creation than we began to delight in that which we shouldn't. This remains one of our characteristics: we can take pleasure in cruelty, selfish-ness, domination, and a whole range of destructive and demean-ing activities. We can effectively delight our way to our own soul's destruction. Augustine's description of this destructive delight conjures up for me the image of Gollum:

---

2. Augustine, *Commentary on the Lord's Sermon on the Mount* 1.12.34.

> So it [the soul] turns away from him [God] and slithers
> and slides down into less and less which is imagined to
> be more and more, it can find satisfaction neither in itself
> nor in anything else as it gets further away from him who
> alone can satisfy it. So it is that in its destitution and dis-
> tress it becomes excessively intent on its own actions and
> the disturbing delights it culls from them . . . .[3]

In their refusal to obey their creator, Adam and Eve turned their
back on unsullied delight. They, in fact, turn their back on the
source of all delight and of their own existence. In so doing, they
begin to face death instead of God—a world of hardship, depra-
vation, and misery is what follows. Genesis portrays humanity as
party poopers *par excellence*.

The fall begins with shame: "Then the eyes of both were
opened, and they knew that they were naked; and they sewed fig
leaves together and made themselves aprons" (Gen 3:7). Prior to
their eating of the tree, Adam and Eve seemed to comprehend nakedness no more than does my dog. In a world without clothes,
what does nakedness mean? Then suddenly and horribly they're
conscious of their own nakedness and that awareness is intimidat-
ing. No longer do Adam and Eve delight completely in each other
and in themselves. The modesty of the fig leaves symbolizes their
shame and, in the shadow cast by that shame, they now discover a
distance between them. The gaze of the other has become threatening and so they must hide themselves. Already perfect love has
been diminished.

Adam and Eve immediately follow this detachment from
each other by hiding in disgrace from God. When God asks them
what they've done, Adam's reply reveals much about what has now
changed: "I heard the sound of you in the garden, and I was afraid,
because I was naked, and I hid myself" (Gen 3:10). Not only has
shame entered into the world but now also fear and the desire to
hide from God. Suddenly, even he has become threatening. They
actually want to hide their own nakedness from the very God

3. Augustine, *On the Trinity* 10.7. Where I have used the word *delights* the
translator uses *pleasures*. The Latin word in the original is *delectationes*.

who created them. The old world of delight has begun to unravel. Shame and fear remain two of the most potent obstacles to delighting in the freedom and generosity God offers us.

God's curses with which chapter three ends describe the world as it is now. In place of the lush garden come the thorns and the thistles, hard labor and pain, and death. "The wages of sin are death" is St. Paul's succinct description of the fall (Rom 6:23). Death and suffering signify the antithesis of abundant life and stand as the obstacle to our enjoyment of it. In all its manifestations, death diminishes delight; death keeps us from being truly free and tempts us to exploit the generosity of others out of either fear or the desperate desire to suck as much juice out of life as we can before we die. The rest of creation now becomes the threatening other, that which must be wrestled with and controlled, and that which must never be trusted.

Just as importantly, fallen humanity is less able to delight in that which is good. We know this instinctively. I'm certainly incapable of constantly delighting in the sun, the air I breathe, the life I've been given, and the flowers I see. I've been known to overlook the occasional daisy or walk right past an elegant butterfly. There are even moments when I don't find my friends and family delightful beyond words. Prayer is often drudgery and worship even worse. I could go on in this vein, but everyone knows this well. If we were capable of delighting in all things, even the small things, we would have no need to pursue happiness because we'd already enjoy it. Thomas Traherne captures this well in one of his meditations:

> Suppose the sun were extinguished: or the sea were dry. There would be no light, no beauty, no warmth, no wine, fruits, no flowers, no pleasant gardens, feasts, or prospects, no wine, no oil, no bread, no life, no motion. Would you not give all the gold and silver in the Indies for such a treasure? Prize it now you have it, at that rate, and you shall be a grateful creature: Nay, you shall be a Divine and heavenly person.[4]

4. Traherne, *Centuries* 1.46

Again, that is the life we were created to enjoy: a communion with our fellow creatures within whose company we are God's priests. As the first chapters of Genesis narrate it, that is the life we forsook by turning away from God.

Because we can no longer enjoy untarnished delight and because the world itself is less delightful than it should be, creation ceases to be that through which we commune easily with God. Certainly, we can still have occasions of exquisite pleasure that make us brightly aware of God's presence. But these are rare moments. Even those who enjoy the beauty of nature know that opportunities for exquisite delight are uncommon and that the unexpected pleasure is never to be enjoyed fully again no matter how much we want to revisit it. For instance, when I was first transfixed by the reflection of the mountains of the Lake District in the still waters of Ullswater my heart danced in a way that it hasn't done there since; the delight I feel whenever I now visit Ullswater, though it remains brilliant, is not quite the same as it was at first. No kiss is like the first kiss.

In fact, if you look at the human condition in light of joy, you can better understand the freedom we have lost through sin. Were we truly free, delight beyond measure would be ours. It would simply be a matter of willing, of intending to enjoy each moment for its own sake, and knowing how go about doing it. But life quickly teaches us that even if we didn't have to contend with the hurt and pain we experience in life, we still couldn't enjoy every moment and every person we encounter. We grow bored and so look elsewhere for new pleasures and delights. G. K. Chesterton recognized this in his inimitable way:

> A child kicks his legs rhythmically through excess, not absence of life. Because children have abounding vitality, because they are in spirit fierce and free, therefore they want things repeated and unchanged. They always say, "Do it again"; and the grown-up person does it again until he is nearly dead. For grown-up people are not strong enough to exult in monotony. But perhaps God is strong enough to exult in monotony. It is possible that God says every morning, "Do it again" to the sun; and

> every evening, "Do it again" to the moon. It may not be automatic necessity that makes all daisies alike; it may be that God makes every daisy separately, but has never got tired of making them.[5]

Variety is the spice of a life that's already impoverished. We lack the freedom to enjoy without distraction and without growing bored. So, happiness becomes something elusive that we pursue through the power of our purses and these days normally with appetites whetted by marketing.

Of course, we don't even need to concern ourselves with always enjoying the blessings of life because we now have the "problem of evil" with which to contend: the tsunamis that slaughter hundreds of thousands, the tornadoes that demolish schools, and the earthquakes that bury cities. Though still a world of plenty, the world is also a place of disease, famine, and drought, a world in which there is so much suffering that we would go mad were we to comprehend even a fraction of it. No, nature can just as easily make us rage against and turn away from God as it can lead us to him. Thus, even if we retained the ability to delight in creation unreservedly, we'd be shocked into cold reality by mere prick of a thorn.

The human response to the delight and danger found in the fallen world is to deify it. Most pagan religions view humanity as totally subject to the capricious mercy of nature (usually embodied by a colorful cast of divine characters), whose every whim must constantly be appeased. From the human sacrifices of the Polynesians to those of the ancient Near East, various religious cultures have viewed nature as a monster to be mollified at great personal expense. Fruitful fields, fertile wives, moderate rains, mild winters, and protection from pestilence all depended on appeals to specific gods or spirits who control or embody parts of the natural world. In his letter to the Romans, Paul gives a theological spin for this anthropological observation:

5. Chesterton, *Orthodoxy*, 60.

> Ever since the creation of the world his eternal power
> and divine nature, invisible though they are, have been
> understood and seen through the things he has made. So
> they are without excuse; for though they knew God, they
> did not honor him as God or give thanks to him, but they
> became futile in their thinking, and their senseless minds
> were darkened. Claiming to be wise, they became fools;
> and they exchanged the glory of the immortal God for
> images resembling a mortal human being or birds or four-
> footed animals or reptiles. Therefore God gave them up in
> the lusts of their hearts to impurity, to the degrading of
> their bodies among themselves, because they exchanged
> the truth about God for a lie and worshiped and served
> the creature rather than the Creator. (Rom 1:20–25)

One of the reasons for this seemingly human compulsion to try to appease nature is that the created order now stands at a distance from us; it is the threatening other. Faced with that complex and encompassing threat, we lose sight of God—the biblical term for this deifying of God's creatures is idolatry. The created order itself becomes the object of our reverential gaze. We worship and serve the creature rather than the creator. At the root of idolatry is the desperate sense of isolation that humankind feels now that we have become disconnected from both God and his creation.

One of the most difficult tasks that Christians face is, therefore, to remind ourselves and others that this unhappy disharmony isn't how life should be. The characteristic modern idea that we are islands, cut off from others and inescapably alone, may give voice to our fallen sense of desolation, but it doesn't describe how things are intended to be. "My God, my God why have you forsaken me?" was the cry of Good Friday, not of Easter. A central part of our ministry as stewards of delight is, therefore, restoring the lines of communication between humanity and God and among human beings. Central to our ministry is sharing in the restoration of God's creation and the reclamation of "Adam's joy and the Temple of his Glory."

Creation's communion with or participation in God is central to this reclamation project. In his poem, "Elixir," George Herbert compares creation to a glass:

A man that looks on glass,

On it may stay his eye;

Or if he pleaseth, through it pass,

And then the heav'n espy.[6]

Creation is supposed to be the lens through which we may look upon and delight in our Creator. Certainly, we may delight in nature itself, just as we might admire a well-made window. But the purpose of a window isn't to be admired but to be looked through; the same is true for creation. A similar approach to creation is expressed through a different metaphor by Bonaventure: "In relation to our position in creation, the universe is a ladder by which we can ascend into God."[7] By discerning the "footprints" of God in the universe, we ascend towards him and come to delight in him through the glory expressed within creation. Creation is the means of that delightful communion with God.

The approach to sin and the fall through the perspective of creation that I've just described alters how one understands the resurrection. It prevents us from taking an overly anthropocentric view of it—as though Jesus' resurrection affects only those who accept Jesus as their savior. To understand what's going on in various stories about Jesus after he has risen, we have to jettison the whole idea that the point of God's plan is to open up the gates of heaven to us and nothing else. That would leave the central problem as presented in Genesis—namely, that we have stopped sharing in God's delightful and generous creation by our failure to be his priestly stewards—without proper resolution. Saying that God achieves victory by placing those who believe in him on a heavenly trophy case would be like saying that the Allies achieved victory when they rescued members of the French Resistance from Nazi-occupied France. Recall that Paul states in Romans 8 that creation is yearning to be freed from corruption; in other words, creation longs to be delightful once more. And this can only happen if humanity becomes God's priestly stewards of delight again.

6. Herbert, "Elixir," ll.9–12. Modernization by me.

7. Bonaventure, "The Soul's Journey into God" 1.2.

The point of redemption, therefore, is to transform the world by restoring humanity to its proper place in creation. In Traherne's language, creation is freed from the "Babel of Confusions" through the redemption of humanity so that it can again become a "Temple of [God's] Glory."

But what might that freedom look like? Jesus' uncanny appearances after his resurrection tell us much about what God is actually doing. In the vivid Gospel accounts, Jesus' resurrected body is neither fully spiritual nor fully natural, at least in any way that we understand nature. He defies that crude dualism. In fact, his body appears to be a union of body and spirit. He does things that are natural: he builds a coal fire and eats fish with Peter and John, breaks bread with the Cleopas and his companion in Emmaus. He joins the eleven in the upper room to eat broiled fish, and, perhaps most memorably, invites doubting Thomas to touch him by placing his finger into his wounds. On the other hand, Jesus can pass through closed doors, is seemingly unbothered by space and time, and has an appearance that has been mysteriously altered.

What we see in these curious stories is a Jesus who has been transformed through the resurrection into something that seems to us both natural and supernatural. Really, he seems to have his own new nature. His resurrection turns out not to be an escape into something completely spiritual as though he had become Jesus the friendly ghost. Nor is it simply an impressive example of resuscitation as in the case of Lazarus. In him we glimpse a new nature, the risen and redeemed nature that has escaped the clutches of death. His body has now been freed from the bondage of death and so is completely free; we see in the risen Christ what freed human nature looks like. In other words, the resurrection isn't about providing a spiritual escape valve from the messiness of material life. Instead, it presents us with a life that has overcome the bondage of death, a life that is totally free. In the risen Christ we witness life too abundant to be limited by death and decay. We see in Christ what it's like to be the kind of totally free human being we are intended to be.

Scripture tends to describe this in terms of different forms of life: in some places, the distinction is made between *psyche* and *zoë* and in others between *psyche* and *pneumatikos*. Although the Greek concept of *psyche* is notoriously difficult to describe, it means something like the inner quality of biological life and thus falls in the vicinity of our own words *soul* and *psyche*. On the other hand, *zoë* refers to a new form of life that somehow surpasses this world. In the New Testament, *psyche* is the life we must lose or transcend. For example, when Jesus was approached by some inquisitive Greeks just before he withdrew to the upper room, he declared: "Very truly, I tell you, unless a grain of wheat falls into the earth and dies, it remains just a single grain; but if it dies, it bears much fruit. Those who love their life (*psyche*) lose it, and those who hate their life in this world will keep it for eternal life (*zoë*)" (John 12:24–25). The former life here is one that's earthbound, terminal, and without freedom; the second breaks free into eternity.

In 1 Corinthians 15:42–47, Paul takes a slightly different approach by contrasting *psyche* with *pneumatikos* but then develops his distinction in a very striking (and often misunderstood) way:

> So it is with the resurrection of the dead. What is sown is perishable, what is raised is imperishable. It is sown in dishonor, it is raised in glory. It is sown in weakness, it is raised in power. It is sown a physical body, it is raised a spiritual body. If there is a physical body, there is also a spiritual body. Thus it is written, "The first man, Adam, became a living being"; the last Adam became a life-giving spirit. But it is not the spiritual that is first, but the physical, and then the spiritual. The first man was from the earth, a man of dust; the second man is from heaven.

Even without understanding precisely what Paul means by physical versus spiritual bodies, we can understand something about their distinction in terms of the Genesis ideal. The physical body is perishable and earthbound; it will return to dust. The second body is imperishable, free, and associated with heaven. Both are bodies—the Greek word *soma* refers to a fleshly body—but they are vitalized differently. Thus, the physical and the spiritual don't pertain to the composition of the bodies so that one is material and the other immaterial. Rather, the contrast is much more like the difference between petrol and diesel engines, describing not the engine's composition but what enables the engine to run. For Paul, the general resurrection is about the fueling of the human body through the spirit of God. Unlike my analogy of the engine, however, this fuel transforms the body in the process.

Admittedly, much of this is beyond our comprehension. But we can draw a little upon our own personal experience to try to understand what these passages are trying to say. One of our hardest balancing acts is to pay equal attention to our body and our spirit. More often than not, they fight and contend with each other. Paul speaks about this in Romans 7:13–25 when he discusses his own flesh and spirit warring against one another so that he can't do what he knows is right. That's the old battle with sin with which we're all familiar. But another way we find the balance hard is that we can either lurch in the direction of our body and become caught up in a materialistic and shallow life or in the direction of the spirit and become so heavenly minded we're no earthly good. In other words, we find it hard not to oppose the physical with the spiritual.

But in the new nature as represented by Jesus, spirit and body work together in inseparable harmony. After our resurrection, to turn our thoughts to the body will be to turn our thoughts to the spirit and to turn our thoughts to the spirit will be to turn our thoughts to the body. The two will be as one. That is the glory of the resurrection and the new creation that follows. In Shakespeare's comedies, the downfall of the villain is followed by a marriage. In our divine comedy, the downfall of the villain death is followed by the marriage of our spirit with our body. And as when a couple come together to form one flesh, so too will our redeemed spirit and our redeemed nature come together to form one delightful body. C. S. Lewis puts it well. The Christian God, he says,

> is the God of corn and oil and wine. He is the glad Creator. He has become Himself incarnate. The sacraments have been instituted. Certain spiritual gifts are offered us only on condition that that we perform certain bodily

acts. After that we cannot really be in doubt of His intention. To shrink back from all that can be called Nature into. . . . Spirituality is as if we ran away from horses instead of learning how to ride. . . . These small and perishable bodies we now have were given to us as ponies are given to school children. We must learn to manage: not that we may someday be free of horses altogether but that someday we may ride bare-back, confident and rejoicing, those greater mounts, those winged, shining, and world-shaking horses which perhaps even now expect us with impatience, pawing and snorting in the King's stables. Not that the gallop would be of any value unless it were a gallop with the King; but how else—since He has retained His own charger—should we accompany Him?[8]

How might this vision of the new creation shape how you understand your ministry? Let's go back to the garden for a moment. What does a garden look like in very early spring? Much of it will appear just as it did in the winter: leafless trees, ground covered in dead, rotting leaves, and flower beds empty of life. But first snowdrops will appear, followed later by daffodils and crocuses. Here and there buds will poke through the cold soil or out from bare branches. Those buds and early blossoms are the harbingers of what's to come. They let us know that before long the garden and the countryside will teem with seemingly new life. If we weren't so inured to the annual transformation of spring, we would find it magical to watch colorful and abundant life emerge from the decay of winter.

As we saw in the first chapter, the image of the garden is one way to express what is happening in Christ's resurrection: as Eden marks the start of creation, the garden in which Mary found Jesus on Easter morning marks the start of the new. Similarly, there is a poetic tradition that has portrayed Christ's resurrection through the image of a flower:

> Christ has flowered in the pure flesh:
> now let human nature rejoice.

8. Lewis, *Miracles*, 194–95.

Human nature, you were so darkened
that you had become like burnt hay!
But your Bridegroom has renewed you
do not be ungrateful for such a lover.

Such a lover is the flower of purity
born in the field of virginity.
He is the lily of humankind,
of sweetness, and of perfect fragrance.

Divine fragrance he has brought us from heaven,
from the garden where He was planted:
This God was sent to us from the blessed Father
a twining of flowers. . . .

The natural color of beauty he had took,
on dire lividness when he was reviled:
He bore bitterness sweetly,
and let his great worth be humiliated.

Mighty worth was brought low,
that breathing flower was trampled underfoot,
surrounded by piercing thorns,
and its great splendor covered.

Splendor that lightens any shade
was darkened by painful grief,
and his light was quite obscured,
in a sepulcher in the flower-garden.

The Flower placed there lay and slept,
it soon came to life again and arose,
blessed body and pure reflowering,
and appeared with great brightness.

A kindly brightness appeared to Magdalen
in the garden who lamented him as dead,
and comforted her in her great weeping,
so that her loving heart was rapt.

> Her heart comforted the brethren,
> and raised up many new flowers,
> and stayed in the garden with them
> with those lambs singing for love.[9]

Christ and the new creation—the latter participating in the former—are the first fruits of a cosmos freed from death and corruption; Christ the "lily of humanity" raises up "many new flowers" in a new garden ringing with God's own love song. In the risen Christ we see creation beginning to spring to new life, blossoming with the abundance of redemptive freedom.

That's where we are right now in the order of things. Abundant life is budding all around us amidst the cold and cheerless parts of our world. Those blossoms of new life tell us what's to come in much the same way that Jesus' resurrection does. When we share each other's love, sacrifice to help someone else, experience the joy of another's recovery, comfort those in need, carry each other's burdens, heal the sick, champion the vulnerable, and (above all) come together in worship and the "breaking of bread," we anticipate that future garden in full bloom. In the early church, these blossoms appeared in the guise of the church's hospitality to all regardless of sex or nationality, the care of widows and orphans, and charity for the poor. Stranger still, it manifested itself in the reported cheerfulness with which the martyrs met their deaths. While we take many of those blossoms for granted now—like hospitals, international laws, innumerable charities, and many of our basic rights—their roots actually reach back to the resurrection and anticipate, however imperfectly, the new Jerusalem. These blossoms also give substance to our Christian hope—the conviction that our world is being completely remade and our reality utterly transformed by Christ's victory spilling over into all creation.

That overflowing of the resurrection reflects the overflowing delight we encountered in the creation story. Because of what Jesus achieved on the first Easter morning, our task as Christians is to share in both God's creativity and redemption. In other words, our delight is to foster and care for God's marvelous creation *and*

9. Iacapone da Todi, "Of the Incarnation of the Divine Word," 13–17.

to restore to health those people and things made less delightful through sin and corruption. The abundant life God offers is both creative and redemptive. The task of giving, nourishing, and redeeming life is what really defines our ministries. Conversely, it's from that vantage that we can see better our vocation to oppose everything that destroys, impoverishes, and corrupts life.

We now live in a world between Easter and the second coming, between the start of new life and its consummation. Now that Jesus has achieved victory over death and corruption, our task is to be buds of abundant life in his new garden. We're to work towards making this world a garden where we can be God's stewards of creative and redemptive delight. We are assured in Scripture that whenever we encourage and nurture those sprouts, our work will enjoy an eternal spring. As the Tom Wright puts it: "You are following Jesus and shaping our world, in the power of the Spirit; and when the final consummation comes the work that you have done, whether in Bible study or biochemistry, whether in preaching or in pure mathematics, whether in digging ditches or in composing symphonies, will stand, will last."[10]

As Wright's quote suggests, there are many different ways in which we can promote the blossoming of God's garden of delight. Throughout the ages, the church has generally identified three broad categories that describe, if you will, the shape and character of God's garden: beauty, goodness, and truth. These are the three main dimensions of abundant life. They may appear in many different shapes and sizes, just as meat, starch, and vegetables may appear on your plate in lots of different forms. Beauty, goodness, and truth, if you will, are the ideals in which we delight and that best point to God's presence in our world. When we promote what is beautiful, good, and true and challenge what is ugly, evil, and false no matter the personal cost, then we can be sure that we're doing our part to restore and promote God's creative delight.

The very exploration of how you can help God to cultivate these buds of the new creation can be one of the most exciting aspects of your ministry. It is certainly what has kept me going and

10. Wright, *The Challenge of Jesus*, 180–81.

provided me with a rich treasury of happy memories. When you adorn your work with prayer and open yourself to God's grace, you'll find that opportunities to recognise and encourage such buds appear constantly. Then, too, you may find that slowly but surely your churches will become like little gardens—only dim reflections perhaps of Eden, Gethsemane, and the new Jerusalem—but gardens all the same where the buds of God's glorious new creation are fed and watered. Indeed, making them such places is why God has called you to be stewards of his delight.

4

Your Ministry and God's Immeasurable Delight

It's remarkable that we find ourselves in a world we generally find beautiful. While I'm sure there are good scientific reasons for this aesthetic awareness, I also think it tells us something about our creator. I suppose God could have created a very different world, one in which beauty either didn't exist or had no impact on us. That's certainly what we humans have often done in our own built spaces as anyone knows who has visited an industrial site or a housing estate built in the '60s or '70s for low-income households. Fortunately, God doesn't seem to be a brutalist because not only did he create a beautiful cosmos but he even made us capable of appreciating, delighting in, and replicating that beauty. Animals don't seem to be aware of beauty. My dog only seems to appreciate beauty when he sits gazing lustfully at my meal—though I doubt it's the comeliness of the snack that occupies his thoughts. Although this point may seem obvious, it's striking that animals, who seem generally to understand comfort and luxury (as demonstrated by the hair on my family's beds and sofa) have no capacity to understand beauty. Only in fairy tales are animals captivated by beauty. So, that's where I'd like to begin: with the notion that the world is beautiful and that we, unlike Whiskers or Fido, are capable of delighting in that beauty.

The opening of Genesis suggests that delight, only writ infinitely larger than anything we've experienced, was involved in God's act of creation. As we saw earlier, the repetition of the phrase "And God saw that it was good" is normally taken to be a moral statement that physical nature is good rather than evil; but it's less often appreciated as God delighting in his own handiwork. God doesn't pronounce the various parts of his creation to be good, as though his declaration is a necessary judgment to make sun, moon, earth, plants, and animals good. He *sees* that they are good. His gazing upon the goodness of creation speaks of appreciation rather than moral judgment. This might just as well be translated, "And God delighted in it." One can almost hear God's playful laughter knitted into the formation of light and darkness, sun and moon, plants and animals. There's a lightheartedness in the opening chapter of Genesis that's often missed. God creates a world that's delightful; his delight is woven into every strand of created existence. In a very important sense, to be delightful to God is to be good and to be good is to be delightful to God.

Then, at the end of Genesis 1 we come to the creation of human beings, man and woman, in the image of God. Over the centuries, much has been made of the biblical concept that human beings bear God's image. Although much of that literature is good, few seem to notice what we actually know about the God when this passage occurs in Genesis 1:26–27. We don't know him yet as a God of judgment or wrath. We must wait for the covenanting God of Abraham and Moses. We don't even know him as the God who will plunge into the depths of human depravity for the sake of our redemption. At this juncture we know him only as a mysterious deity who seems to delight in creating. We also don't know at this stage *why* God creates: simply that he does and that he delights in it. So, when he unexpectedly makes Adam and Eve in his own image, what might that mean? At this point in Genesis the only image we have of God is as a mysteriously generous creator of delightful things. That suggests to me that fundamental to this strange idea that we are made in the image of God is the idea that like him we should also create and delight in good things.

If this is so, it shouldn't be surprising that God not only creates Adam and Eve but also gives them dominion over this strange world of wonder. If you leave aside for a moment the moral tone of the story of creation (as important as that is), your eyes are opened to an astonishing world. What are we to make of this playful God who seemingly delights in the excesses of life—"swarms of living creatures" is how the New Revised Version puts it—and then with equal delight creates humanity to reflect his own playfulness and have dominion over his playground? It's all rather astounding when you consider it. Thomas Traherne catches this sense well in his poem, "Eden":

> Joy, pleasure, beauty, kindness, glory, love,
>
> Sleep, day, life, light,
>
> Peace, melody, my sight,
>
> My ears and heart did feel, and freely move.
>
> All that I saw did me delight.
>
> The Universe was then a world of treasure,
>
> To me an universal world of pleasure.[1]

Implicitly, the creation narrative of Genesis 1 speaks to the almost reckless abandon of God's free generosity that, in turn, demonstrates his divine delight: a delighting God speaking into existence a delightful world. We might almost say that creation springs from God's laughter.

Notice, too, the one command God gives in the first chapter of Genesis: "Be fruitful and multiply." It's the only command we humans have happily and enthusiastically obeyed. Again, we see here God's playfulness. He could, I suppose, have formed a static world in which the swarms of living creatures never procreated but simply existed. That's, in fact, how some early church fathers imagined it. Instead, God, who apparently doesn't have a Victorian bone in his body, tells the multitudes of varied life to come together and produce new life. There's a joyful lushness in Genesis 1 that reveals much about God. What the theologian David Ford says about joy describes God in the first chapter of Genesis just as well: "There is something explosive, excessive, and overflowing about joy that resists containment. There can even be a wildness,

1. Traherne, "Eden," ll.15–21.

a sense that life is not domesticated and predictable . . . ."[2] There ought to be a hint of this wild delight whenever we speak of God as creator lest we be tempted to put a leash on him and make him overly refined.

So, it's fitting that after capping off this new world with a garden, God's first worry, the first time his delight is diminished, is when he says, "It is not good that the man should be alone." So far, everything God has done has been good and wonderful. There's not an ounce of regret or timidity in Genesis 1. In Genesis 2 one gets the sense that God almost made a mistake for suddenly in verse 18a he sees something that isn't delightful: Adam is alone. Unless humanity can also share in conjugal love, the world won't be utterly delightful. And so God fashions Eve; her formation completes humanity and caps the perfect world.

That act of creation also forms a family bond not only between God and his creatures but also amongst the creatures themselves. You may be a much more complex and capable organism than lichen, but both you and lichen share the same Father: God. We and every creature are, therefore, siblings; each of us relate to God as Father according to our natures. Two people who celebrated the fellowship of all creation were Aelred of Reivaulx and Francis of Assisi, both devoted to the religious life. Aelred wrote a lovely little book called *Spiritual Friendship* in which he exalts friendship as the highest expression of love. He makes much of the fact that God created nothing to be alone. Of rocks and trees, he writes, "what soil or what river produces one single stone of one kind? Or what forest bears but a single tree of a single kind?" Similarly animals "imitate man in this regard to such an extent that we almost believe they act with reason. How they run after one another to play with one another, so express and betray their love by sound and movement, so eagerly and happily do they enjoy their mutual company that they seem to prize nothing else so much . . . friendship." Above human being, the angels also share in a "pleasant companionship and delightful love" that makes them one in will and desire. Finally, Aelred calls attention to Eve's

2. Ford, *The Shape of the Living*, 180.

creation from Adam's rib, which he suggests teaches us that "human beings are equal and, as it were, collateral, and that there is in human affairs neither a superior nor an inferior, a characteristic of true friendship." All creation, therefore, shares an "implanted desire" for fellowship that unites every creature: "He has willed . . . that peace encompass all his creatures and society unite them; and thus all creatures obtain from him who is supremely and purely one, some trace of that unity. For that reason he has left no type of beings alone, but out of the many has drawn them together by means of a certain society."[3]

St. Francis is, of course, famous for his concern for the natural world. His earliest biographers recounted his affection for animals. One of my favorite stories is how Francis would "ransom" lambs about to be slaughtered as a way of expressing his gratitude to the Lamb of God.[4] But nowhere is Francis's view of the world better expressed than in his "Canticle of the Sun," where we find a holy delight in what God the Creator has done:

> Praised be you, my Lord, with all your creatures,
>
> especially Sir Brother Sun,
>
> Who is the day and through him You give us light.
>
> And he is beautiful and radiant with great splendor;
>
> and bears a likeness of You, Most High One.
>
> Praised be you, my Lord, through Sister Moon and the
> stars;
>
> in heaven You formed them clear and precious and
> beautiful.
>
> Praised be You, my Lord, through Brothers Wind
>
> and through the air, cloudy and serene, and every kind
> of weather
>
> through which You give sustenance Your creatures.
>
> Praised be You, my Lord, through Sister Water,

---

3. Aelred of Reivaulx, *Spiritual Friendship* 1:53–58.

4. Bonaventure, "The Life of St. Francis," 8.6.

> which is very useful and humble and precious and
>   chaste.
>
> Praised be You, my Lord, through Brother Fire,
>
> through whom you light the night
>
> and he is beautiful and playful and robust and strong.
>
> Praised be You, my Lord, through our sister Mother
>   Earth,
>
> who sustains and governs us,
>
> and produces varied fruits with colored flowers and
>   herbs.[5]

Here, the whole family of creation is united through our shared praise of God. Francis almost perfectly expresses what it means to be stewards of God's delight. In his poem, humanity serves as creation's high priests including all creatures in its love of God's creatures and giving voice for them to the praise of our shared creator.

Francis's poem, however, reminds us that we aren't entirely like our brothers and sisters. In Genesis, unlike the "swarms of living creatures," Adam and Eve are given a job: they're told to have dominion over the world. What are we to make of this dominion? When my son was old enough for me to begin reading him stories (a delight I now sorely miss), I searched the bookstores and Internet for a good children's Bible. This was much more difficult than I had anticipated. Many turned out to be nothing more than the Authorized Version sentimentally illustrated with Biblical characters apparently fresh off the sunny beaches of California. Finally, I settled on one Bible that had charming pictures, the main stories of the Old and New Testaments, and chapters brief enough to hold a three-year-old's attention. To my surprise, however, the moral of the second chapter was that God had created all the plants and animals simply to be used by humankind, as though without us the world would have been pointless. There was no hint at all that God freely created the cosmos to delight in it. Instead, according to this take on Genesis, all the delights of creation have only one purpose: to be a resource for human exploitation. One wonders

5. Francis of Assisi, "Canticle of the Sun," ll.3–9.

why the authors didn't update God's proclamations to read: "And God saw that it was useful"! I immediately checked to see if the publisher was a multinational oil corporation.

Nowhere in Genesis does it suggest that God created his world of delights primarily to be used for our own needs or desires. The world is not one big factory and shop combined into one for our benefit. The world would be no less good and delightful if God had saved himself a lot of trouble and stopped his work before creating humanity. He didn't say before the end of the sixth day, "I see that it will be good once I create humankind to utilize its many resources." God created the world to be something in which he can delight and that can both receive and return that delight. As Augustine declares about creation, "God saw that it was good; it was out of the same genial courtesy, after all, that he took pleasure in what had been made, as that it had pleased him that it should be made."[6] In other words, God delights in the intention, act, and the results of creating. He is like a craftsman who is first intrigued by an idea for a new work, then enjoys actually crafting it, and finally admires his handiwork once it's completed—except that with God the intention, creation, and delight are all one. In that respect, our use of God's work of delight is entirely secondary to his delight; indeed, our use of the earth should be such that God will delight in our use of it: not unlike a toy maker taking pleasure in watching a child play with the toys he has so lovingly constructed.

That God was pleased to make a world in which he could delight suggests that divine delight is woven into the very fabric of creation. More than almost anyone else, Augustine recognized this fact about our existence. He believed that delight isn't just an emotional response but actually exists within the Trinity itself; indeed, he identified it most closely with the Holy Spirit, whom he called "blissful delight."[7] Since everything that's good depends on God's goodness for it to be good, then so too does our delightfulness partake of God's own delightfulness. To be good is to be delightful or, better, to share in God's own delight. In one of his sermons on

6. Augustine, *Unfinished Literal Commentary on Genesis* 1.8.14.

7. Augustine, *On the Trinity* 6.12.

the Psalms, Augustine writes, "But there is a simple good, sheer Goodness-Itself, in virtue of which all things are good, the Good itself from which all good things derive their goodness. This is the delight of the Lord, this is what we shall contemplate."[8] In other words, our very existence (which is what it means to be good) is rooted in God's own delight.

If we hold Augustine's approach to delight together with Aelred and Francis's notion of the fellowship of all creatures, then we begin to glimpse how creation is supposed to be a communion of delight. Each of us exists only through God's delight—all creatures are effectively delighted into existence—and, therefore, we are united by this shared origin, manifesting in our individual ways the fact that God sees that we are good. Surely, a little of this lies behind Matthew 6:25–34 when Jesus commands us not to be anxious about tomorrow since God takes care of the birds in heaven and the lilies of the field; both the birds and the lilies please God as much as we do and are equally objects of his love. But they have a different purpose than we do. Birds fulfill God's intention by singing their melodies, building nests and being fruitful; lilies by growing into beautiful, fragrant flowers. But what about us? How do we share in the created community of delight in such a way that we participate more fully in God's delight? I believe it's by faithfully fulfilling our call to have dominion over the earth. But we have to understand that dominion aright.

Rowan Williams points out that in Eastern Orthodox teaching Adam's naming of the animals is seen as a priestly blessing.[9] In ancient Middle Eastern cultures, people believed that names held power. This idea lies behind the Old Testament ban on saying God's name. By giving Adam responsibility for naming the animals, God allows him to participate in the playful act of creation. That responsibility also makes Adam take creation seriously. He can't just look on life as a faceless mass of living creatures. To name each fish, bird, and land animal properly, he must relate to that creature, understand it, and t7ake pleasure in it. He can't simply

8. Augustine, *Exposition of the Psalms* 26 (2), 9.
9. Williams, "Changing the Myths We Live By," 177.

look at animals in terms of their usefulness to him—that would be like naming one's child Dishwasher or Mower—he has to do it in terms of that animal's own existence as a concrete example of God's own delight.

The garden of Eden represents humanity's relationship with creation. Since Eden is the world's holy of holies, it symbolizes the best of what God has created. There, Adam and Eve live harmoniously with God and with the world around them. They are the gardeners of God's delightful estate. This ideal is expressed wonderfully by Augustine when he imagines what life must have been like for Adam and Eve: "You see, there was no stress or wearisome toil but pure exhilaration of spirit, when things which God had created flourished in more luxuriant abundance with the help of human work. As a result the creator himself would be praised more abundantly."[10] What could be more sublime than humanity praising God through its playful task of assisting him to bring abundance to all life? Anyone who has felt the satisfaction of gardening has tasted a little of what this joy might be like.

All of this is to say that creation is sacramental: it's an outward and visible sign of the otherwise hidden beauty and delight of God. Indeed, if creation reveals God as Paul states in Romans 1, then beauty and delight reveal God's own beauty and delight; they give us a hint of the supreme beauty and delight that are God. In other words, creation participates in God's own delight and that makes it delightful. In the words of the theologian Ken Leech, "the universe is the form in which the beauty of God manifests itself. The sacraments of sun, moon, sea, and earth, bird and beast are completed by the sacrament of man, the climax of the creative process."[11] C. S. Lewis echoes this sentiment when he writes in his imaginary letter:

> I had thought one had to start by summoning up what we believe about the goodness and greatness of God, by thinking about creation and redemption and "all the blessings of this life." You turned to the brook and once

10. Augustine, *The Literal Meaning of Genesis* 8.15.
11. Leech, *True Spirituality*, 95.

> more splashed your burning face and hands in the little
> waterfall and said, "Why not begin with this?"
> And it worked. Apparently you have never guessed
> how much. The cushiony moss, that coldness and sound
> and the dancing light were no doubt very minor bless-
> ings compared with "the means of grace and the hope
> of glory." But then they were manifest . . . . They were
> not the hope of glory, they were the exposition of the
> glory itself.[12]

This sense is one of the greatest gifts of sacramental Christianity.
The use of fruits of the earth—water, bread and wine, and oil—as
means of grace serves to ground people in the created order and
to hinder them from spiraling off into overly cerebral forms of
religiosity. This earthiness is particularly encouraged in Catholic
worship, with its use of bread and wine, beeswax, fire, precious
metals, salt, and incense. Here we see humankind functioning as
creation's high priests, offering back to God what he has already
offered to us.

How far removed this myth is from the gospel of industrial
Christianity. It was awfully convenient for people during and after
the Industrial Revolution to portray dominion as domination and
to exaggerate the command to subdue the earth. This was the myth
on which were built William Blake's "dark, satanic mills" and by
which the air, sea, and land could be blithely poisoned. Indeed,
consider how much our way of life depends on producing ugliness:
industrial wastes, toxic rivers, floating masses of discarded plastic,
sweat shops, and shanty towns practically drowning in their own
filth. Too much of what we consider good today—such as access
to a wide variety of cheap goods, comfortable homes, and copious
leisure time—depends to one degree or another on others enduring shocking ugliness. The modern myth has also allowed for the
commodification of every part of nature, including human beings.
We live now in a world in which we must "sell ourselves," develop
"winning" personalities, and spend vast sums of money improving
ourselves both physically and emotionally. How much time and

12. Lewis, *Letters to Malcolm Chiefly on Prayer*, 88–89.

money do we spend in the desperate hope that others will delight in us? Rowan Williams argues that we must discard this myth not because of some naïve and romantic belief that the earth is benign and always cooperative, but because even after Adam and Eve were chucked out of Eden, creation remains a gift in which we are to delight, commune with God, and share with others.[13] Our proper use of the world and the way we relate to one another should continually reflect our God-given delight.

But that's the rub, isn't it? Obviously, we have to make use of the world and its resources. Farming and industry are the bedrocks of human civilization, not to mention necessities for human life. In the Genesis story, even God makes use of the world's resources when he provides Adam and Eve with animal skins to wear (demonstrating that he isn't above a little tailoring himself). But this shouldn't be much of a dilemma. We've all had experiences of receiving gifts that are also useful. One of the ways we show our gratitude is by taking good care of the gift itself. Parents know this well. How many times have we said to our children, "If you break that toy, you won't get a new one"? There are ways to make use of creation that honor that creation. That's what separates *use* from *abuse*.

That we even see usefulness and delight as opposing each other shows how far we have to go. J. R. R. Tolkien put all this memorably in a letter he wrote to a fan. In it, he distinguishes between what he calls "magic" and "art." Magic, what he also calls the "Machine," is the use either of our own talents or of other creatures "with the corrupting motive of dominating: bulldozing the real world, or coercing other wills."[14] In *The Lord of the Rings*, Saruman exemplifies magic: he demolishes the world around him in order to form his army of monsters. Indeed, he tears down trees simply to tear them down. He stands as a metaphor for the Industrial Revolution. The Elves of Middle Earth are his opposite: they are great artists and craftsmen who live in harmony with their surroundings, upholding what is good, enduring, and ennobling. Tolkien writes that the object of their magic is "Art not Power, sub-creation not

13. Williams, "Changing the Myths We Live By," 177.
14. Tolkien, *The Letters of J. R. R. Tolkien*, letter 131, p. 145.

domination and tyrannous re-forming of Creation."[15] Their meat and drink are myth, song, poetry, the arts, and fine craftsmanship; all activities little esteemed by us who have grown accustomed to mass produced goods and services.

In other words, God wants this world to be a place of astonishing delight; he wants us to be astonishingly delightful people. In many ways, God's desire is encapsulated by Jesus' claim in his parable of the Good Shepherd: "But I came that they may have life, and have it abundantly" (John 10:10). Certainly, this is a messianic claim, but it's also a job description for humanity's role within creation. That is, if you will, the touchstone by which we judge our actions, decisions, and our ethics. How do our actions—both individual and collective—encourage an abundance or flourishing of life? What ideas and practices discourage such flourishing or even diminish life? To encourage and nurture the former and challenge the latter are, therefore, central tasks of the church.

Before I suggest some ways that the church's ministry might do that, we need first to look a little more closely at delight itself. The first thing to note at this point is that delight and the encouragement of delight aren't extraneous details. Again, the reason why God's delights in his creation and weaves delight into the fabric of all his creatures is that God himself is delight. Remember God always is what he has: God isn't just wise, he's supreme wisdom itself; God isn't just merciful, he's supreme mercy itself; God doesn't just love, God *is* love. So also, God is supreme delight. Augustine refers to God as infinite delight, an idea echoed by Anselm who calls God "immeasurable joy" who fills every atom of our being.[16] For Augustine, delight is most closely associated with the Holy Spirit—to have the Holy Spirit poured out into our hearts is to be filled too with God's own delight. Similarly, Julian of Norwich's conviction that God's delight pervades everything is what allows her to proclaim boldly, "all shall be well, and all shall be well, and all manner of things shall be well."[17]

15. Ibid.

16. Anselm, *Proslogion* 25.

17. Julian of Norwich, *Showings*, 13.27.

Fundamentally, delight is *enjoying something for its own sake*. Delight is devoid of expectation and demand. It springs from the simple pleasure that something exists rather than doesn't. That's what makes delight completely different from entertainment. Entertainment has to stimulate us in order to remain entertaining; it distracts us. Delight, on the other hand, takes us deeper into the world around us. It involves a sort of communion or communication between that which pleases and the person who is pleased. Aquinas refers to this communion as "expansion" whereby our affection reaches out to the object of our delight "as though it surrendered itself to hold within itself the object of delight."[18] If I delight in a wildflower, for an all too brief moment I connect through something—an intuition, a feeling, call it what you will—with that flower. Love is present.

Now you may object and dismiss the whole idea of loving a wildflower as little more than sugary sentimentalism. One may enjoy its beauty, but to say that one loves the dainty blossom is going too far. And were this merely a material world with no creator, I think this argument would have merit. I may find the idea of people pledging their eternal love to wildflowers very appealing (and think the world would be far better for them) but such is not normal behavior. But if you believe in a creator then a whole new dimension appears. I may not in the midst of delight love a wildflower in the same way I love a fellow human being, but something akin to love caused me to stop, notice the flower, and devote my attention to it. Augustine stated boldly that there is no love without delight and I would argue that the reverse is also true—there is no delight without love. Because I believe that God created that wildflower, imbuing it with gentle beauty, I believe also that he, in a sense, wove grace into its atomic structure. My delight in the flower's graceful beauty gives me a taste of God's own grace and beauty and that experience engenders love. Perhaps the reason for this is that God wove the same grace and beauty into me. In that sense, perhaps our appreciation of beauty and goodness in the other is really a resonance between the delight woven by God in us

18. Aquinas, *Summa Theologica* I–II, q. 33, a. 1.

both. Now, because I'm far from perfect, that communion or res nance may only be fleeting—I may even tread on the poor plant as I walk away—but that doesn't speak to the nature of my delight or my love, simply to my inability to sustain that state for very long.

But such delight is unreciprocated. Perhaps in a way utterly alien to us, a wildflower "delights" in sunshine or refreshing rain and exhibits that delight through the rich color of its flowers. But it's completely unaware of me when I admire that color. It cannot delight in me. That in no way diminishes my own delight since I'm enjoying the flower for its own sake and it, in a sense, communicates back to me through its natural beauty. But delight is magnified when it's reciprocated. When I delight in the God who delights in me, grace abounds. When I delight in the company of those who delight in me, strong bonds of affection are formed. And when we share in the delight of those who also delight in God, we experience *koinonia*, the deep communion by which God dwells in each of us and we in him. Anselm speaks of this *koinonia* of delight when he writes,

> But surely if someone else whom you loved in every re-
> spect as yourself possessed the same blessedness, your joy
> would be doubled for you would rejoice as much for him
> as for yourself. If, then, two or three or many more pos-
> sessed it you would rejoice just as much for each one as
> for yourself, if you loved each one as yourself. Therefore
> in that perfect and pure love of the countless holy angels
> and holy men where no one will love another less than
> himself, each will rejoice for every other as for himself.
> If, then, the heart of men will scarcely be able to compre-
> hend the joy that will belong to it from so great a good,
> how will it comprehend so many and such great joys?[19]

In such a joyful communion, the self is overwhelmed by the light of the doubling delight as we participate in God's enjoyment of our rejoicing in those who rejoice in us and we and them in him. As Julian of Norwich writes, "God rejoices in his creatures and the creatures in God, endlessly marvelling, in which marvelling they

---

19. Anselm, *Proslogion* 25.

see their God, their Lord, their maker, so sublime, so great, and so good in comparison with them who are created that they seem hardly to exist at all."[20]

But if delight is enjoying the other for its own sake, then our own delight can't be predicated on others delighting in us; our delight shouldn't be caused by others delighting in us (as much as that may help) since it then becomes self-referential and, therefore, no longer delight. Indeed, I suspect one requirement for holiness is the ability to delight in those in whom no one else delights and who may find us insufferable. At the same time, however, I believe Anselm is right to say that delight is doubled when it's shared. His view was likely informed by Augustine's idea that true delight involves love that is actually the Holy Spirit dwelling within our hearts. So, when we share in each other's delight, we share in the bond of the Spirit who is the delight of the Father and the Son. In other words, a communion of delight shares in and expresses the communion of delight that is God the Father, Son, and Holy Spirit. Richard of St. Victor describes this when he writes,

> After all, when two mutually loving persons embrace one another with supreme longing and are delighted in each other with supreme love, then the supreme joy of the one is in the intimate love of the second, and, conversely, the excellent joy of second is in the love of the first. As long as the first person alone is loved by the second, then he alone seems to possess the pleasures of his excellent sweetness; similarly, as long as the second does not have a third mutually loved person, then he lacks a communion of excellent joy. But so that the two persons can communicate such pleasures, they must have a third mutually loved person.[21]

When we enjoy one another for each other's sake—in effect, losing ourselves in each other—then we come closest to imitating and revealing the nature of the Trinity; we also come nearest to enjoying the free generosity from which we were created and by which

20. Julian of Norwich, *Showings*, 16.44. My modernization.
21. Richard of St. Victor, *On the Trinity*, 3.15.

we have been redeemed. It is then that we can begin to show others what it means to be a new creation and discover freedom.

How, then, do you introduce such delight into your ministry? First, trying to be delightful yourself wouldn't go amiss. At its best, the evangelical tendency to emphasize the joy of God in conversation and worship has a quality of this. Such delight can also be found in a more quiet way among contemplatives who can subtly express God's delight without having to say much of anything. Obviously, some people will by nature and good fortune be more well-disposed towards displaying such delight. But everyone can become objects of delight through a little honest self-reflection and the love they try to show to those around them. This obviously takes grace, but what is grace but the substance of God's delight poured out on us? Moreover, if you haven't already, try to be keenly aware of how eager others are to delight in you. In my experience, the majority of people actually want to delight in their ministers. We too often make this harder by failing to love, or hiding away in our offices, or working too hard to be pious. Just learning to listen attentively and with open hearts is often enough to encourage others to delight in you. There's not an atom of divine earnestness in the story of creation; there shouldn't be any in your ministry either.

Secondly, make delight the hallmark of how you serve your people. *Enjoy them for their own sake.* We can so easily relate to members of our congregation in terms of their usefulness (always thanking Ms. Jones for making coffee after church but hardly ever talking to her as a person) or in terms of their potential or shortcomings. We can also too easily fall into the trap of never expressing delight in our sermons and prayers. If we constantly remind people of their shortcomings or address the world's sufferings in our intercessions (as important as they are), we can end up expressing a world view that is, frankly, depressing. Western churches in particular fall into this trap by speaking about little else than the plight of the suffering and oppressed. Those are vital concerns and cannot be forgotten or ignored, but you do them little good if you can't bring them and the people you address out of the darkness of despair and into the hopeful light of God's delight.

So, make sure that you regularly remind those to whom God has sent you that you delight in them (however hard and requiring of deep prayer this may be). It is then that your love and care for the *real* them—warts and all—will begin to lead them towards the God who delights in them for their own sake.

More importantly, try to open the eyes of those God places in your care to his inexhaustible delight. It's no good doing this through some cheap appeal to entertainment—that's just a distraction from true delight. Rather, help them to enjoy God, creation, and each other for their own sake. So much of our relationship with God is based on expectation: on the often unarticulated conviction that God does something for us, be it the promise of peace and security or the hope of heaven. But that belief never rises above relating to God in an adolescent fashion; loving and delighting in him for what he does for us rather than for whom he is. The motto of St. Chard's, my college at Durham University, is "*non vestra sed vos*" ("not yours but you"), and this speaks directly to the kind of delight that we can teach those to whom we minister. It's by learning to enjoy God, creation, and each other for their own sake that we begin to discover God's freedom and generosity.

Finally, stand up to and challenge the many sources of ugliness in the world that diminish delight. We live in a world that increasingly makes delight more difficult because we settle instead for often tawdry and relentless entertainment that drowns out the quiet moments when we can encounter delight. Moreover, our willingness to destroy God's creation through waste, pollution, and unsustainable consumption makes us less disposed to appreciate delights if we do encounter them. Included here is also the ugliness of war, economic exploitation, abusive relationships, and the experiences and relationships that lead people into self-destructive habits and mental turmoil. Finally, while there is so much suffering and malice in the world, we feel less free to delight. How can one in conscience delight in a field of wildflowers when others fields are being filled with the graves of innocent dead? Delight compels us to confront the viciousness of human life and seek to overwhelm it with God's delight. Central to the task of serving as stewards of

God's delight is doing just that: tearing out the weeds of evil and corruption and sowing the same ground with the buds of God's new creation.

Being delightful, helping others to delight, and making our world more delightful describe a great deal of the Christian vocation. None of these activities would be possible if God did not delight in us. We delight because God first delights in us. That delight is a deep delight woven not only in our DNA but into the atomic structure of the whole cosmos. It's a very mystical delight, beyond our comprehension but not our experience. And so, I can think of little that is more inspiring and hopeful than the idea that God delights in us through and through and that when we reach the goal of our salvation we will undoubtedly hear the Father echo his words at Jesus's baptism by declaring: "These are my children in whom I am well pleased."

_____ 5 _____

Your Ministry and the Love of God

To SERVE AS GOD's image-bearing priesthood of the new creation by becoming open to God's free generosity through which you have been made delightful and can delight in him, your neighbors and creation for their own sake—that is the vocation to which you have been called. You are, through God's grace, to be a blossom of the new creation, showing through your life and love what the paradise of God's kingdom is like and will be like when it's fulfilled. In a real sense, through your ministry you are planting a flag of God's kingdom in your area reminding people under your pastoral care that, however imperfectly, God's new creation is to be seen all around them. And the way that you do that is by conducting your ministry in light of the resurrection and in anticipation of Christ's second coming. The inaugurated life of the new creation and its consummation when Christ returns flow from both time past and time future to make God's abundant life present in the ordinariness of pastoral ministry. In effect, it's our task to share the life of the resurrection and of the new creation to everyone we meet. That task is fundamentally what is meant when we say that the church has a ministry of love for what else is abundant life than the love of God?

That is also where we run into the most difficulties. My old ethics professor used to say that God created us in his image and we've been returning the favor ever since. Just as we want to create God in our own image, so too do we want to define love in our own way. That impulse is even more problematic in an age when, thanks in part to heaps of popular songs and films, we have reduced love to a sentiment. That saccharine version of love may be awfully good for selling music and greeting cards, but it doesn't do us much good when we're confronted with real life. The relationship between real love and its sentimental version is like that between the reality of caring for a baby and the fantasy of it being mainly about adoring a cute little "bundle of joy" all the time. It's also like the difference between actual marriage and the sentimental version of it we see in films. We may be attracted by the charming versions but experience teaches us that the actual thing, though much harder to pull off, can ultimately be much richer and more satisfying.

Because *love* has become such a loaded word and idea, I'm hesitant even to use it as the culmination of my reflections about God and delight. Saying that our faith is fundamentally about love has been one of the most effective ways of emptying our faith of all power—our understanding of the love of God becomes focused on engendering a feeling, perhaps through doing something good and useful, but self-referential all the same. Moreover, almost anything challenging can be explained away by claiming that it isn't loving. In his inimitable way, Stanley Hauerwas calls our attention to this:

> Nothing is more destructive to the Christian faith than the current identification of Christianity with love. If God wants us to be more loving, why do you need Jesus to tell us that? And if Christianity is about the forgiveness of our sins, then why did Jesus have to die? If God is all about love, in other words, why go through the trouble of being this man, Jesus? Why did God not just tell us through an appropriate spokesman (it could have been Jesus) that God wants us to love one another? God, in such a faith, becomes that great "OK" who tells us we are OK and, therefore, we are taught we should tell one another we are OK. But if Jesus is the proclamation of the great OK, why would anyone have bothered putting him to death? There must have been some terrible failure in communication.[1]

1. Hauerwas, "What's love got to do with it?"

If we do no more than express the idea of love in terms of how we feel (or ought to feel) or of how accepting of others we may be (or ought to be), we really don't do God's love justice. Indeed, it can become a means for inactivity, keeping us from seriously and honestly engaging with others as they really are; love rooted in popular ideas about tolerance and respect is a cold thing indeed.

But love isn't about being nice and respectful; it's not a matter of how inclusive and open-minded we are. Nor is it measured by the views we hold or even by the particular works we do. I think one of the reasons why Paul describes love in 1 Corinthians 13 in such an exalted fashion is to remind the Christians of Corinth that true love is utterly beyond them. There's no way to realize in our own lives anything like the Pauline description of love simply by working hard to love others better or to have a more inclusive attitude towards them; loving properly and truly is a matter not of training but of grace, though it still requires hard work. Part of the reason for this is that love is rooted in and reveals the free generosity of God in which the old self is lost as the new self is formed. In other words, the Christian understanding of love always contains within it the pattern of Christ's own ministry: the self-emptying of the incarnation, the death of the cross, the triumph of risen life, and the elevating glory of the ascension.

Love, therefore, requires a willingness to give away our precious selves (and what is more dear to us?) so that we may receive new selves as we grow up together in Christ. Because love involves dying and rising, Paul says of himself, "It is no longer I who live, but it is Christ who lives in me. And the life I now live in the flesh I live by faith in the Son of God, who loved me and gave himself for me" (Gal 2:20). In other words, love is rooted paradoxically in death. This is one of the scandals of our faith: that the only way we achieve true life is by starting with the shock of death. I'm not referring here to the physical death we all will one day experience, so that God's love and life remain undiscovered until we enter heaven. Rather, we encounter God's love and life by daily embracing death to our own selves. "If any want to become my followers, let them deny themselves and take up their cross and follow me.

For those who want to save their life will lose it, and those who lose their life for my sake will find it" (Matt 16:24). That is what God's love looks like when we truly encounter it in our lives.

If the Christian understanding of love is rooted in death and denial, then it should go without saying that it's not easy. But growing into the love of God by walking the way of the cross is the only way we can become those new creatures who have discovered the freedom, generosity, and delight of God. We have to let go of ourselves to discover true freedom, we have to be released from our enslaving fears to be truly generous, and we have to be caught up in others in order to delight in them. Part of the reason for all of this is that our old selves—dominated by fear and self-centered desires—stand in the way of God's love. The former Archbishop of Canterbury, Michael Ramsey, speaks of this when he writes, "By the power of the Spirit who brings the self-giving of God into the convert's life the self-centered nexus of appetites and impulses is broken, and the life is brought into a new center and a new environment, Christ and His Body."[2] But this is only to say that our experience of God's love conforms to the pattern of death and resurrection and of creation and new creation. New life arises from old life not by our own efforts but by our sharing in Christ's death—at the threshold of old and new life stands the cross:

> For the love of Christ urges us on, because we are convinced that one has died for all; therefore all have died. And he died for all, so that those who live might live no longer for themselves, but for him who died and was raised for them. From now on, therefore, we regard no one from a human point of view; even though we once knew Christ from a human point of view, we know him no longer in that way. So if anyone is in Christ, there is a new creation: everything old has passed away; see, everything has become new! (2 Cor 5:14–17)

By being incorporated into Christ, we become a new creation through whose veins God's generosity, freedom, and delight

---

2. Ramsey, *The Gospel and the Catholic Church*, 33.

flow—this is just another way of saying that in Christ we become vessels of God's love.

As compelling as Paul's vision is, it should also give us pause since a transformation that conforms to the image of the cross can't be an easy one. For this reason, Scripture can speak of love as having a searing quality as though it burns away those aspects of us that separate us from God, however dear they may be to us. Undoubtedly, this arises from the identification of the Holy Spirit with the tongues of fire at Pentecost. Love is also challenging, prodding, and even overwhelming as captured famously in John Donne's poem:

> Batter my heart, three person'd God; for, you
>
> As yet but knock, breathe, shine, and seek to mend;
>
> That I may rise, and stand, o'erthrow me, and bend
>
> Your force, to break, blow, burn and make me new.[3]

It's the love of God that compelled Abraham to leave all behind and cross the desert to Palestine; the love of God that required Joseph to undergo slavery and imprisonment before rising to the heights of Egyptian power; the love of God that allowed his people to be taken into exile; and the love of God that brought them back. Most of all, it was God's love that embraced our sinfulness and took upon himself our corruption and self-destructive tendencies by being crucified. And it was the love of God that burst death apart on Easter morning.

But the love of God runs deeper than just through the actions of God. It's not just a matter of observing what God has done and does and then seeking to discern his love in those acts, however hard that may be to perceive at times. In other words, we shouldn't speak about love as though it were only a quality of God's good and generous activities. First, that makes us the judge of what love is and absurdly puts God in the chair of the accused, having to explain to us how his activities meet our criteria for love. Our own experiences or the shock of great tragedies may tempt us to do just

---

3. Donne, "Sonnet 14," ll. 1–4.

that, but we need to resist that urge, for down that road lies only despair or self-righteousness. The more important reason that we must not see God's love only as an attribute of his actions is that God doesn't just do loving things, he is love: "God is love, and those who abide in love abide in God, and God abides in them" (1 John 4:16b).

Augustine provides one of the most attractive approaches to understanding how God might be love. Poor Augustine has come under attack in recent years for his Trinitarian theology. Whatever his shortcomings may or may not be, he provided an understanding of God as love that profoundly shaped the spirituality of Western Christianity. In his great work on the Trinity, he proposed the image of the triune God as Lover, the Beloved, and the Love shared between them. The Father loves the Son who receives and returns the love of the Father; the binding love shared between them is the Holy Spirit. Augustine writes, "Now love means someone loving, and something loved with love. There you are with three, the lover, what is being loved, and love."[4] In other words, if God is perfect love then every aspect of love is found in him. Because God is perfect love, he needs no other (as we saw in chapter two) because Father, Son, and Holy Spirit supremely are love. As Anselm argues in his *Monologion*,

> suppose that no other creature existed, i.e. suppose that nothing else had ever existed, other than the supreme spirit. That Father and the Son would still love themselves and each other. It follows from this that Love is nothing other than the supreme essence (i.e. what the Father and the Son are).[5]

Love is the very essence of the God we worship; it's not just a way of understanding his actions but is his very nature. God is the love that Father, Son, and Holy Spirit share and he is the love he pours into our hearts and into every nook of his creation.

---

4. Augustine, *On the Trinity* 8.14.

5. Anselm, *Monologion*, 53.

But because the New Testament links love especially with the Holy Spirit, Augustine wants likewise to identify the Holy Spirit in a special way with love:

> Then that inexpressible embrace . . . of the Father and the Son is not without enjoyment, without charity, without happiness. So this love, delight, felicity, or happiness . . . is the Holy Spirit in the Triad, not begotten but the sweetness of the Begetter and the Begotten pervading all creatures according to their capacity with its vast generosity and fruitfulness, that they may keep their right order and rest in their right places.[6]

In other words, the loving communion shared between the Father and Son is the Holy Spirit. Now, much of this lies beyond our imagination (and some theologians quibble with what they do understand), but don't worry about that. Just allow the image of the eternal Lover, the eternal Beloved, and the eternal Love appeal to your imagination. That God himself is love means, among other things, that love is ultimate and eternal. If we ever lose sight of that fact in our personal beliefs or in the teachings of the church, we lose sight of God himself.

There are two important consequences of the idea that God is love. First, it means that love is the source of all created existence. Julian of Norwich recognized this when she exclaimed that God "made all things that are made for love, and by the same love they are preserved and will be without end."[7] Love also has to be the basis for everything because God, who is love, is the ground of all being. We see this idea in the last quote from Augustine where the sweetness of the Holy Spirit pervades everything with its "generosity and fruitfulness." The reason why creation delighted God in Genesis is because it was created out of his love. In other words, the fundamental fabric of the whole universe isn't an array of cold, unrelenting laws, but the love of God. In his *Paradiso*, Dante imagines the cosmos as being unified by God's love:

---

6. Augustine, *On the Trinity* 6.11.

7. Julian of Norwich, *Showings* 7.15. My modernization.

> I saw how it contained within its depths
>
>   all things bound in a single volume of love
>
>   of which creation is the scattered leaves:
>
> how substance, accident, and their relation
>
>   were fused in such a way that what I now
>
>   describe is but a glimmer of that light.[8]

And he ends his great work by singing about the "the Love that moves the sun and other stars."[9] What we see only as laws through our scientific lenses, Dante saw as love.

Likewise, the love of God creates all things, sustains all things, and provides all things with order. Aelred of Reivaulx writes,

> This love sustains and contains all creatures, leaving nothing in disarray, nothing in disorder, nothing without some appropriate plan and place. Love is the heat of fire, the cold of water, the clarity of the air, the opaqueness of the earth. Love binds and joins all these quite opposing elements in all corporeal creatures, so that nothing is joined together improperly; yet the disparate natures of these elements are not destroyed.[10]

Love has us surrounded and pervades us entirely; separation from that love doesn't mean loneliness and separation—really it means annihilation. To try to live without God's love would be like trying to exist apart from our atoms.

Second, if God is love, then he becomes present in a particular way whenever love is present in an active and intentional way. In that sense, we might define any action of love as making God present. Again, this is something Augustine understood well:

> Let no one say, "I don't know what to love." Let him love his brother, and love that love; after all, he knows the love he loves better than the brother he loves. There now, he can already have God better known to him than

8. Dante, "Paradiso," Canto 33.85–90.

9. Ibid., Canto 33.134–35.

10. Quoted in Sommerfeldt, *Aelred of Reivaulx*, 1.

his brother, certainly better known because more present, better known because more inward to him, better
known because more sure. Embrace love which is God,
and embrace God with love. This is the love which unites
all good angels and all the servants of God in a bond of
holiness, conjoins us and them together, and subjoins us
to itself. . . . And if a man is full of love, what is he full
of but God?[11]

Seeking to love others, then, becomes a primary form of evan-
gelism because it makes God really and truly present not only in
both the lives we affect and our own lives but also in the very act
itself of loving. This is the reason why Jesus compels us to feed the
hungry, satisfy the thirsty, welcome strangers, clothe the naked,
care for the sick, and visit prisoners; his striking statement, "Truly
I tell you, just as you did it to one of the least of these who are
members of my family, you did it to me" (Matt 25:39), reveals to
us the intimacy of God's love shared between neighbors and God.
Actions of love might even be called eucharistic in that they make
God present in a special way or rather allow us to participate in a
special way in the presence of God who never stands apart.

God is love, we were created from and are sustained by God's
love, and we become especially aware of God's presence whenever
we love. Love finds its first home in God. Writing in the twelfth
century, William of St. Thierry put it this way:

Concerning the love of which we are treating, one ought
not to conceal its birth; from where it takes is lineage
of eminent nobility. . . . Its birthplace is God. There it
is born, there nourished, there developed. There it is a
citizen, not a stranger but a native. Love is given by God
alone, and it endures in him, for it is due to no one else
but him and for his sake.[12]

But we mustn't forget that God's love also redeems us. "God so
loved the world that he gave his only Son that none who believe
in him should perish but have everlasting life" (John 3:16). Paul

11. Augustine, *On the Trinity* 8.12.
12. William of St. Thierry, *The Nature of Dignity of Love* 1.3.

speaks of this when he declares in Romans that "God shows his love for us in that while we were still sinners, Christ died for us" (Rom 5:8). This famous passage comes immediately after he declares that by enduring suffering we encounter a hope on which we may rely "because God's love has been poured into our hearts through the Holy Spirit who has been given to us" (Rom 5:5). The same love through which we were created and by which we exist became one of us and died upon the cross for our redemption. The love that formed us comes to us in our self-imposed exile to return us by his love to the God who is love so that we may be enfolded more fully into his love by the reception of the Holy Spirit. That not only sums up our faith but it also roots and defines our vocation as stewards of God's delight.

Yet, for all that, we can be strangers to the love that created, sustains, and redeems us. God is nearer to us than we are to ourselves and yet we are often entirely blind to him. Pure unalloyed love is a stranger to us, even though Love knows us intimately. Augustine laments this is in *Confessions*:

> Late have I loved you, beauty so old and so new: late have I loved you! And see, you were within and I was in the external world and sought you there, and in my unlovely state I plunged into those lovely created things which you made. You were with me, and I was not with you. The lovely things kept me far from you, though if they did not have their existence in you, they had no existence at all. You called and cried out loud and shattered my deafness. You were radiant and resplendent, you put to flight my blindness. You were fragrant, and I drew in my breath and now pant after you. I tasted you, and I feel but hunger and thirst for you. You touched me, and I am set on fire to attain the peace which is yours.[13]

Here again, God's love is forceful and searing. There's an erotic quality to God's love that awakens within us a deep desire. That longing is also a longing for God's freedom, generosity, and delight. To be in bondage to sin means to be separated in some way from love

---

13. Augustine, *Confessions* 10.27.

and, therefore, also from freedom, generosity, and delight. Again, this isn't a complete separation as we would then cease to exist. In reality, our separation from God's love is a self-imposed fantasy, a pretense that we can somehow go our own way apart from that love. A key ingredient of our redemption, therefore, is waking up from that fantasy and learning to recognize the intimate closeness of, and our total dependence on, God's love.

Fortunately, as Augustine's quote indicates, love isn't passive but seeks us out constantly. Though Augustine and others often spoke about the first experience of God's love using violent terms such as "burning" and "breaking," they generally preferred less coercive terminology in describing how God's love seeks us out. For them, God is more like a wooer than a conqueror. And it's precisely in describing how God's love woos us that they turned to the idea of delight. Their logic went something like this:

Love and delight depend absolutely on each other. Augustine stated this in one of his sermons when he declared that someone "only loves, after all, what delights one."[14] This is echoed by Aelred, who argued, "Where there is no love, there is no delight. . . . The greater the love for the highest good, the greater the delight and the greater the happiness."[15] So, we can't be coerced into loving God since such force would make love onerous and drain it of all delight. The only way God can gain our love, therefore, is to convince us to delight in him and his ways. But as I said in the last chapter, because we are fallen we no longer have the capacity dependably to delight as we ought; indeed, we have the tendency to delight in that which we shouldn't. Lacking freedom and generosity, we respond to God's call with fear, feeling that God's love demands too much of us, requires us to be more vulnerable than we can accept. God needs to overcome our self-protective barriers without using force so we can encounter his love and begin to delight in him.

This is where the Holy Spirit appears. If the Holy Spirit is in some particular way both the love and delight of God, then he is key to our being able to respond openly and positively to God.

14. Augustine, *Sermons* 159.4.
15. Aelred of Reivaulx, *The Mirror of Charity* 1.4.10.

We need God's own delight in the form of the Holy Spirit in order for us not just to delight in God but crucially *to want* to delight in him. In Romans, Paul claims, "God's love has been poured into our hearts through the Holy Spirit that has been given to us" (Rom 5:5). When we receive that love through the outpouring of the Holy Spirit we also receive God's delight and consequently we begin to desire to share in God's love, generosity, and freedom. We become new creations not against our will but because through the reception of the Holy Spirit we now want to be renewed.

A helpful way to think about this is in terms of an eloquent speaker. Imagine yourself as part of an audience that's initially hostile to the speaker. The speaker, however, is incredibly charming and eloquent and radiates goodwill. Despite yourself you come to be captivated by her; you want to be on her side, to agree with what she believes. Her words gradually work their magic so that by the end of the speech, almost without realizing it, you have been completely swayed. Her ideas now please you and because they please you, accepting them feels right, feels like the thing you yourself want to do. Similarly, God is like a charming lover: the Holy Spirit is his charm that speaks directly to our heart and through love and delight woos us to him. Because our hearts have been filled with his delight, we now want to do as he wills. Like romantic love, the wooing itself leads to even greater delight so that in our conversion we become smitten. Gradually, we come to be pleased by doing what pleases God. It's then that we discover the free generosity that he offers and can begin properly to delight in him, our neighbors, and his creation. In that sense, sanctification is just another way of saying that we are becoming increasingly charmed by God.

But we mustn't forget that even after we've received the Holy Spirit into our hearts, we remain apart from God in our sinfulness. Indeed, the delights of those sins compete with God's delight, so that our growth into the love of God can often be painful. Traditionally, the presence of the Holy Spirit in us has been compared to a fire that draws us closer to God; the fire of the Holy Spirit fills our hearts so that we begin, like a hot air balloon, to ascend to God. Sin acts like a weight that pulls us back to earth and away from God. And so the Holy Spirit pursues different avenues to fill us ever more with God's love, coming to us in prayer, Christian fellowship, worship, even the simplest acts of love, and the Eucharist, the sacrament of love.

Two well-known poems express what I've been describing about God's love in remarkably compelling ways. The first is George Herbert poem, "Love (III)":

> Love bade me welcome: yet my soul drew back,
> Guilty of dust and sin.
> But quick-ey'd Love, observing me grow slack
> From my first entrance in,
> Drew nearer to me, sweetly questioning,
> If I lacked any thing.
>
> A guest, I answer'd, worthy to be here:
> Love said, You shall be he.
> I the unkind, ungrateful? Ah my dear,
> I cannot look on thee.
> Love took my hand, and smiling did reply,
> Who made the eyes but I?
>
> Truth Lord, but I have marr'd them: let my shame
> Go where it doth deserve.
> And know you not, says Love, who bore the blame?
> My dear, then I will serve.
> You must sit down, says Love, and taste my meat:
> So I did sit and eat.[16]

Here, Herbert presents us with the vision of Love himself gently approaching the protagonist (presumably Herbert himself) and tenderly convincing him to be welcome. In his sinfulness, he draws back, even though he secretly wants to be included. He doesn't feel like he's deserving and finds reasons why he can't or shouldn't be allowed to belong. But Love doesn't accept his excuses. Unworthy? Love doesn't think that for a minute. Blind? "Who made the eyes but I?" Marred? "Who bore the blame?" Finally, with no excuses remaining, the author submits and is welcomed by Love to

16. Herbert, "Love (III)." Modernized spellings by me.

"taste my meat": the Eucharist, which is nothing other than the very substance of Love. Love beckons the author, convinces him to remain when he tries to turn away, and gives him a space at Love's table where he can be nourished by love. Love has him surrounded and Love tenderly refuses to let him fall away into despair and self-loathing.

The second poem is the much sung hymn "*Discendi amor santo*" by the rather obscure fourteenth-century poet Bianco da Siena:

> Come down, O love divine,
> seek thou this soul of mine,
> and visit it with thine own ardor glowing;
> O Comforter, draw near,
> within my heart appear,
> and kindle it, thy holy flame bestowing.
>
> O let it freely burn,
> till earthly passions turn
> to dust and ashes in its heat consuming;
> and let thy glorious light
> shine ever on my sight,
> and clothe me round, the while my path illuming.
>
> Let holy charity
> mine outward vesture be,
> and lowliness become mine inner clothing;
> true lowliness of heart,
> which takes the humbler part,
> and o'er its own shortcomings weeps with loathing.
>
> And so the yearning strong,
> with which the soul will long,
> shall far outpass the power of human telling;
> for none can guess its grace,
> till Love create a place
> wherein the Holy Spirit makes a dwelling.[17]

17. Bianco da Siena, "Come down, O love divine."

I know of no other work that so perfectly expresses all the aspects of the love of God discussed in this chapter. It is a poem as worthy of our deep, prayerful reflection as of our singing in worship. In the first stanza, we call on the divine love to descend into our hearts to fill us with the fire of the Holy Spirit. In the second, we long for the fire of love to burn away the dross that separates us from God so that we can be clothed in God's radiance. In the next stanza, love itself becomes our outward clothing and humility our underclothes. Finally, love and grace intertwine with our longing and desire to create within us a home for the Holy Spirit. The images of fire, light, spirit, humility, grace, and human yearning all combine poetically to impart of powerful image of divine love that's almost erotic in the way it tries to tug at our deepest longings. And the underlying theme of the hymn speaks of our transformation by spiritual love into new creatures; in the final stanza we become God's temple filled with the Spirit and, therefore, also with God's love. Whenever we sing this hymn it becomes our individual and collective prayer that God would satisfy our restless hearts with his ardent love.

It should be clear at this point that to be stewards of God's delight is also to be stewards of God's love. The intimate connection between love and delight is such that they can never really be divided. Learning to delight in God, our neighbors, and in creation is the same thing as learning to love them (and vice versa). The Christian ministry, therefore, is fundamentally about seeking through our service and words to open up the world around us to God's loving delight. In its self-centeredness and fear, humankind has ceased to be a willing receptacle of God's love. We are called by God to draw people by love to Love through our acts of love. But even after we have received the Holy Spirit and have become part of the new creation, we have much growing into the love of God ahead of us. We still avoid God's freedom, shy away from his generosity, and refuse to believe that we ourselves are delightful. We still too often assist in making the world around us less delightful and stand in the way of our neighbors flourishing in God's love.

Similarly, too often when we speak about the love of God in our churches, our words lack depth and richness. We've become too enamored with buzzwords like *inclusivity, respect, tolerance,* and *acceptance*; while all these are undoubtedly good, they don't even begin to plumb the depths of God's love focused as they are on attitudes. Worse still, lacking such richness and depth, our expressions of divine love become almost indistinguishable from what people encounter elsewhere in the world. We present ourselves as halfhearted lovers and then wonder why we're such poor wooers. Part of the reason for this is that unless we embrace the free generosity that will allow us to express God's love, we'll continually fail to relate to and connect with others on more than a surface level. How many of our churches are too much like a collection of unconnected masks that hide the richness of the individual lives, desires, and foibles that are contained within the inward self? God calls our churches to be temples of God's love where we discover true love by sharing in God's love present within and among his people. To do that, we must know each other.

My favorite image for a church that takes seriously the love of God and our need to grow up and into that love is *schola caritatis*: a school of love. By means of the Holy Spirit, empowered by God's grace, and within the body of Christ, we must learn to set aside our old selves and embrace our new selves formed in Christ and rooted in God's generosity and freedom. Our churches need, therefore, to become schools of love where people can learn the customs and manners, as it were, of their new home: the new creation where heaven and earth are united and where the faithful can never be separated from the love of God: "Neither death nor life, neither angels nor demons, neither our fears for today nor our worries about tomorrow—not even the powers of hell can separate us from God's love. No power in the sky above or in the earth below—indeed, nothing in all creation will ever be able to separate us from the love of God that is revealed in Christ Jesus our Lord" (Rom 8:38b–39). How we can help our congregations to become schools of love for the stewards of God's delight will be the subject of my final chapter.

6

Schools of Love, Schools of Delight

SOMETIME BETWEEN 1125 AND 1141, Aelred of Reivaulx's personal hero and more famous contemporary, Bernard of Clairvaux, wrote a short treatise entitled "On Loving God," in which he sought to answer the question "how much God should be loved."[1] Although Bernard wanted to give a concise reply—"The reason for loving God is God; the measure, to love without measure"—he felt constrained to offer more for the sake of the "unwise."[2] That he wasn't able to give a short response on the topic of love isn't surprising given that he was in charge of the Cistercians, a monastic order dedicated to the love of God. So, asking him about the love of God was a bit like asking a statistician about baseball or a conductor about classical music—Bernard's friend had to have known he wouldn't receive a pithy reply.

In "On Loving God," Bernard imagines the experience and practice of loving God as a kind of ascent from a weak and "carnal" form of love to one that is really a union with God. Medieval writers loved describing the Christian life in terms of ladders, steps, and stages. Bernard was no different. His stages of love are a kind of ladder of sanctification whereby the faithful climb ever closer to the God they are learning to love. While I find the medieval

1. Bernard of Clairvaux, *Bernard of Clairvaux,* 70. In general, I have used Pennington's translation because it is smoother and uses more inclusive language. Unfortunately, since key passages are omitted, at times I have used the translation from the Classics of Western Spirituality series and have indicated when this is the case.

2. Ibid.

ladders to heaven a little too tidy and systematic, I think Bernard's description of the four stages of loving God provides a helpful way of understanding pastoral ministry in light of what I've been discussing in this book.

Before Bernard discusses his four stages of loving God, he first argues that the highest form of love is to love God for his own sake. In his opinion, that is our aim as human beings. It's important to keep that goal in mind as we turn to Bernard's stages of growth in love because otherwise it's easy to misunderstand him. I'll explain what I mean in detail later, but now I want to focus on the goal of loving God for his own sake. As I discussed in chapter 3, loving God for his own sake is the same as delighting in him, enjoying him not for what he offers us but for who he is. So, according to Bernard, the highest goal of human existence is to delight fully in God. Such delight is the end of our sanctification, the grace-filled route by which we enter into a right relationship with God. Bernard believes that God deserves our love because he first loved and delighted in us. In other words, our own love is but a small token of the love God has already shown us; we return to God a mere speck of what he has given us. Bernard explains,

> First see in what measure God deserves to be loved by us, and how he deserves to be loved without measure. For . . . "he first loved us." He loved—with such love, and so much and so generously—us who are so insignificant and who are what we are. I remember that I said at the beginning that the way to love God was to love without measure. Now since the love which is directed to God is directed to something immense, something infinite. . . . Who, I ask, ought to draw a line to our love or measure it out. . . . So immensity loves; eternity loves; love which passes understanding gives itself; God loves, whose greatness knows no bounds, whose wisdom cannot be counted, whose peace passes all understanding, and do we measure our response?[3]

3. Bernard of Clairvaux, "On Loving God," 6.16.

Yet, as Bernard's stages imply, measuring our own love is precisely what we do. We lack the freedom and generosity to return to God what he has so liberally given us. And so, somehow we have to learn to be free in our response, to let go of the fear, anxiety, and self-centeredness that keep us apart from God, so that through loving him properly we might be sanctified by love. By delighting in God we draw closer to God's own delight; in Bernard's view, ultimately we lose ourselves in that delight.

This growth in the delightful love of God through learning to love him without measure is fundamentally what the Cistercians meant when they described their monasteries as a *schola caritatis*, or a school of love. In that "school," the monks were taught humility, which was understood to be the soil in which the seeds of love might bear fruit. So, they ordered their corporate life on the *Rule* of St. Benedict, interpreting it in such a way that love and humility were emphasized. Moreover, by rooting love in humility, the Cistercians were expressing their belief that growth in the love of God involves dying to self-interest. In a letter Bernard had earlier written to the "Holy Brothers of Chartreuse," he explained,

> There are some who praise God for his own power, some who praise him for his goodness, and some who praise him simply because he is good. The first is a slave, fearful on his own account. The second is a mercenary, and desires profit for himself. The third is a son who honors his father. Both he who is fearful and he who is greedy act for themselves. Only he who loves like a son does not seek his own.[4]

You might think of Bernard's love as God-directed selflessness; it is learning how to give yourself so freely to God that you lose yourself entirely. Only by such self-surrender do we then discover our true selves in the love of God and life of Christ.

I think it's important to elaborate on this last point since it's so easy to misunderstand what is meant by losing oneself. Especially among some Eastern religions, one may find the pious ideal that ultimately we should become totally absorbed in the divine. In some

4. Ibid., 12.34.

ways, this was the Neoplatonic belief and one that clumsily made its way into some examples of early Christian theology. But, as we saw earlier, the Christian ideal is not that salvation involves losing ourselves so entirely that the self dissolves into God; rather the process of forsaking ourselves paradoxically allows us to discover our true selves. So, when someone like Bernard speaks about self-surrender what he has in mind is the surrender of the old, rebellious self after which we come to discover who we really are; in terms of love, you might think of this as discovering yourself in intimate communion with others rather than in some "splendid isolation" from them. Our problem is that we've been taught too well to think of our true self as someone standing at distance from others, that somehow to be authentic we need to be freed from the impinging interests of those around us. I suppose Bernard would have been horrified by such a thought; to him that would have been to erect a dismally small and claustrophobic prison cell for ourselves.

The first rung of Bernard's ladder of love is our loving ourselves for our own sake. "This is carnal love," he writes, "by which we love ourselves above all for our own sake. We are only aware of ourselves."[5] This is like a baby who loves her parents for what they provide: milk, warmth, swift response to demands, and a reliable change of diapers. This is the need-love that I discussed in chapter 2. Bernard doesn't dismiss such love as only selfish and self-centered. For him, it's the natural place for fallen people to begin. Gradually, however, this bodily love grows into a love of neighbors as we learn that we can't meet all of our own needs; eventually, our self-love "overflows" into a love for our neighbors. And so, in Bernard's scheme, bodily love "becomes social when it is extended to others."[6]

The next rung of the ladder is when we learn to love God for our own sake. This partly happens because we discover how hard it is to love our neighbors and how much they are incapable of satisfying our needs and desires. Bernard imagines that these insights arise when God sends us "tribulations": God wills "by a deep and salutary counsel that we be disciplined by tribulations, so that

5. Bernard of Clairvaux, *Bernard of Clairvaux,* 71.
6. Ibid., 72.

when we fail and God comes to our help we who are saved by God will render God the honor due to him."[7] We turn to him in crisis and sorrow and earnestly beg for his love, strength, and perhaps even a miracle. In this stage, we're like teenagers who suddenly show their parents love and affection when they want cash or a lift to a concert. It represents growth, but remains self-centered. I think this is where Bernard imagines most people end up.

But some discover how to love God for his own sake and this is the third rung of the ladder. It comes about, suggests Bernard, as we frequently and repeatedly experience "God's liberation" in the midst of crisis. This can't help but awaken love in our hearts. Bernard asks if we are frequently freed from crises by God, "must we not end, even though we had a heart of stone in a breast of iron, by realizing that it is God's grace that frees us, and come to love God not only for our own sake but because of who he is?"[8] Loving God for his own sake is an act of adoration, when we love God with all our heart, mind, and strength without expectation of profit. This is, if you will, when we discover his freedom and generosity and bask in it. Bernard writes, "Our frequent needs oblige us to invoke God more often and approach him more frequently. This intimacy moves us to taste and see how sweet the Lord is. Tasting God's sweetness entices us more to pure love than does the urgency of our needs."[9] Bernard calls such love free because it shares in God's own freedom. By giving back what God has given us, we discover how to love as God loves us: that is, to love unstintingly. Bernard explains, "This love is pleasing because it is free. . . . Whoever loves this way loves the way we are loved, seeking in turn not what is our own but what belongs to Christ, the same way Christ sought not what is his own but was ours, or rather, ourselves."[10] Finally, because this love is so pure and free, it can't help but spill out of us into our neighbors through a kind of exuberance we discover from tasting the "sweetness of the Lord."

7. Ibid., 73.
8. Ibid., 73–74.
9. Ibid., 74.
10. Ibid.

Finally, we reach the highest rung of the ladder of love when we discover how to love ourselves for God's sake. "To lose yourself, as if you no longer existed, to cease completely to experience yourself, to reduce yourself to nothing, is not a human sentiment but a divine experience."[11] Bernard describes this stage as being drunk with God: so ecstatic is the experience that he admits it can be tasted only briefly before the general resurrection when the faithful become perfectly united with God. Now worldly concerns and our need to love our neighbors weigh us back down to earth. This final stage is only reached by those men and women we call saints and so, on this side of the grave, remains more of an ideal or guiding light than anything we can really know and experience fully. In Bernard's words, it becomes the thing that we "desire" above all else.

Whenever I have taught Bernard's scheme, students have been surprised that loving God for his own sake is the third rather than the final step. After all, earlier he had said that loving God for his own sake is the highest form of love. The best way to understand what Bernard is describing is to think of loving God for his own sake as a two-staged process. The first stage is adoration and the second consummation or an ecstatic union with God; in the first, we focus our attention on God for his own sake; in the second, we lose ourselves in him and his love. Bernard compares this to a drop of water in wine, molten iron in a fire, and radiant light: "It is deifying to go through such an experience. As a drop of water seems to disappear completely in a big quantity of wine, even assuming the wine's taste and color, just as red, molten iron becomes so much like fire it seems to lose its primary state, just as air on a sunny day seems transformed into sunshine instead of being lit up, so it is necessary for the saints that all human feelings melt in a mysterious way and flow into the will of God."[12] But lest we think that this is some kind of ecstatic self-annihilation, Bernard is quick to add that our identity will remain though under another form, glory, and power. Again, we'll discover what it means to be ourselves in intimate relation to God and others rather than in standing apart from them.

11. Ibid., 75.
12. Ibid., 76.

Now, it's always well to remember that the man who wrote these lovely words could himself be a first-rate ass. But the Bible is filled with God working marvels through first-rate asses, which should give hope to all ministers. Again, I'm not sure the scheme is actually very helpful for individual people, except perhaps as an aspiration. The idea of love being a ladder one can assiduously ascend certainly doesn't accord with my own experience, which is characterized much more by the law of undulation with many peaks and troughs and without much sense of movement forward or backward. And I certainly wouldn't advise you trying to chart the people you serve on a *Bernard of Clairvaux Spectrum*! But, while I think his advice was overly optimistic in terms of individuals, I think there just might be something to it in terms of our churches.

Accordingly, the first stage of love can be taken to describe congregations who love themselves for their own sake. They know a kind of love, but for all their apparently Godward worship, their energy and attention are almost entirely directed towards themselves. The scope of their ministry may be to maintain the church building, so that they are really a sanctified historical society. Or their ministry may consist primarily of organizing social events like fundraisers, civic ceremonies, bingo nights, and the like. Although such congregations may also be good at looking after active parishioners, their energy is chiefly aimed at ensuring the survival of the church and the defense of preferred forms of worships and popular social events. In popular parlance, these are "maintenance" churches that exist almost solely for the purpose of continuing to exist. What one doesn't find in their midst is much evidence of the free generosity, delight, and abundant love of God.

Now, one needs to be a little careful here. There is now a large body of literature devoted to attacking such places as inert if not dead. But I think there is often a vital kind of love that needs to be recognized in these otherwise barren places. First, there is usually a love born from familiarity that exists among the active members of the congregation. They've likely known each other for a long time and have been brought closer together through their devotion to the church. However much that devotion may be a headache to you (and often it's expressed through unhelpful cliques and narrow-mindedness), you may need to recognize the kind of love that expresses itself in familiar bonds of mutual affection. Second, circumstances may make evidence for God's free generosity, love, and delight hard to provide—three old ladies, an octogenarian veteran, and a cat struggling to raise funds to keep the doors of the church open isn't much to work with! But more than once in my own ministry, I've seen even in such dead places just enough love to spark a small flame if nurtured properly. Finally, often in such places, the people themselves can see how futile their devotion has been and yet they still come faithfully and still give their time and energy to maintaining worship and trying to look after each other. I suspect in such seemingly pointless devotion, Christ is more present than in many seemingly prosperous churches.

All the same, whether through narrow-mindedness or circumstances, such places have become too inwardly focused and self-interested to be obvious buds of the new creation. Many of them are too much like early buds hit by a late frost—there is no hope for them other than to shut them down and to try to graft them onto a new church community. Other churches, however, may be able to grow to the next stage of love if cared for properly and diligently. Often this comes by their finally surrendering and admitting that on their own they'll never succeed. By gently prodding such congregations to think about their neighbors—not just within the parish but elsewhere as well—and injecting a regular dose of good humor, energy, and optimism, and by revealing to them through sermons and conversations the hope of the new creation, one may help them to begin to love God for their own sake. This obviously requires a great deal of work and energy and not a little patience. My own experience is that such places typically come to life not through the sudden conversion of the current active membership but by a compassionate performance of the ministry that draws new people into the church. This is where the dismissive attitude towards "bums on seats" is unhelpful; often the only hope for a church is a sufficient increase in membership formed in a new and appealing vision of the kingdom of God to change the whole culture of the church. In such places, the lay and ordained ministers would do well to direct their energies towards forming new membership into a visible community of the new creation without pastorally neglecting those who have diligently kept the church open.

If successful, such places can become communities where God is front and center and where people do have energy, perhaps even a sense of mission. You can go far with these kinds of churches—far enough, in fact, that you can mistake them for the real thing. But at this stage, they love God only for their own sake. What might that look like? First, churches that love God for their own sake typically insist that God be worshipped as they want to worship him. This worship might be formal, liturgical worship with all the trappings of catholic ceremonial or it might be lively, nonliturgical worship with praise music and engaging talks and testimonials. Nothing may be wrong with either form of worship (or anything in between) except that the worship itself becomes an object of devotion. When the *form* of worship is allowed to take priority over the mission of the church to be stewards of God's delight then people begin to expect that God approves of and will conform to their "style" of Christianity. In such places, worship itself becomes a kind of baptized lifestyle accessory that seeks to appeal to people's aesthetic tastes rather than draw and form them into the life of God.

Communities that worship God for their own sake also identify themselves too much against other kinds of Christians—those nasty traditionalists, those close-minded evangelicals, those godless liberals, etc.—and begin to view them as part of the "problem," whatever that "problem" may be. A horrendous amount of energy is wasted by churches today either out-shouting opposing groups within the church or expressing fears about their aims and methods. One of the most identifying characteristics of those who seek to be stewards of God's delight is a willingness to try to delight in those with whom they *least* identify. What else is the incarnation than God identifying totally with those who had most estranged themselves from him? Christ's incarnation and crucifixion set the pattern whereby we seek to identify and even sympathize with those we find most unappealing. So, no matter how large or financially prosperous a church is, when its life is too deeply shaped by its advocacy of a particular narrow and probably party-political approach to God, then it has much growing in the love of God yet to do. Churches do less good when they champion a particular position within the surrounding culture than when they're able to take people to some extent beyond that culture to connect with an alternative vision for human flourishing. As I've argued throughout this book, we aren't introducing people to what life within the new creation is like then we are falling short of the graced ministry to which we've been called.

Finally, churches that still only love God for their own sake typically rely almost entirely on their clergy for vision and so-called leadership. The reason for this is that the people of God have yet to be seized by God's call for them to be stewards of his delight. Likely, their understanding of Christianity either remains stuck in the old paradigm of doing what's necessary to get into heaven or else defines clergy or lay leaders as godly gurus who dispense guidance for wholesome living. The former type often loses sight of the church's role in nourishing sources of delight and challenging the ugliness of the world. The latter often neglects salvation itself, forgetting that life within the new creation can't be contained with the narrow confines of bourgeois expectation; God's love is too powerful and expansive to be reduced to form of religious self-help guidance. Moreover, in both cases, the laity sit, often in a way that rarely challenges them, on the sidelines of the church's ministry instead of sharing fully in the mission of the church to introduce people to God's new creation. In the end, like the seeds in Jesus' parable, churches that love God for their own sake also quickly collapse at the first crisis or when they discover to their surprise that their clergy are only human.

In some ways, these congregations are harder to move along than the first type. The first type mainly needs additional numbers and a few active people who aren't well-advanced in years to begin showing signs of transformation. In contrast, the second type of church often succumbs to institutional pride. They start to think of themselves as successful and, indeed, may often been presented as examples to others, especially if they're financially prosperous. But don't be fooled. What they still haven't found is their collective vocation to be God's image-bearing priests, to be those signs of the new creation that can call those still entangled by the "thorns and thistles" of this world into the delight of God's kingdom. There is all the difference in the world between a church that functions successfully as a nonprofit organization and one that is actually a beacon of the new creation.

Your main task in churches that love God for their own sake is to get them over themselves and their own narrow definition of Christianity so that they can begin to love God for his own sake. Expand their vision of the gospel and their love for God so that their love for their neighbors becomes rightly oriented and directed. Show them in the conduct of your ministry—the way you love them, the conversations you share with them, and the challenging teaching you provide them—the freedom, generosity, and delight to which God calls them. In short, free them from the worst bondage of all: the bondage of their own opinions. This will only happen, though, if you encourage them constantly to become lively servants of God—actively seeking to be the buds and blossoms of the new creation to the people they encounter. I've found that a teaching ministry is key here since so many even active Christians have benefited from only a limited formation into the narrative of Scripture or an understanding of the vocation to which they have been called in their baptism. So, their encouragement into a vitalizing Christian identity needs to be continuously expressed through your sermons, teachings, the formation of children and adults, and through the way they are taught to care for one another. They also need to be taught to understand worship not as an activity to meet their individual needs and tastes but as the defining act of the church whereby they offer themselves totally to God so that through word and sacrament they may encounter his freedom and grace. It's by such activities that your congregations may learn to love God for his own sake, to delight in him, and thereby become astonishing places of abundant life.

Imagining how to be a church whose life manifests the freedom, generosity, delight, and love of God is extremely difficult in an age that emphasizes organization and method. So many books on church ministry mistake organizational health, determined largely by criteria devised for businesses, for the main thing. They seem to suggest that as long as churches thrive organizationally—for example, have healthy finances, efficient administration, and successful membership campaigns—then they are serving the ends to which God has called them. These organizational aspects of local churches are important, but they can easily obscure the vocation of churches to be outposts of the new creation. In fact, organizational models can be very efficient at disguising the free generosity of a God who delights as much in human weakness and foibles as he does in their effectiveness. Similarly, slavish conformity to methods of ministry may produce ministers who impress others with their confidence and acumen but do little to show people an alternative way of living. The attempt to confine the ministry to particular rationalized models is a strangely modern obsession that has done much to drain the ministry of charm. I believe one of most unbecoming habits of the historic church has been the way that it has constantly tried to confine the wildness of God's overflowing freedom and love within the power structures of the world, be that the medieval aristocracy, enlightened gentry, or the businesspeople and CEOs of today.

Like Bernard with individuals, I don't believe it's possible on this side of the second coming for congregations to reach the final stage of love. Frankly, I find it hard even to imagine what congregations that lose themselves so fully in God that they forget themselves entirely would look like. I imagine a church that had learned to love itself solely for the sake of God would be one where outsiders would find themselves in a topsy-turvy community, where the life they encountered would make sense only by perceiving that its life had to be drawn from elsewhere. Such a church would live corporately in a way that demonstrated the freedom of God without yielding to shallow permissiveness, the delight of God without settling for vapid entertainment, and the love of God without caging it within ideology or political stances. The people there would have discovered, perhaps not without regular stumbles, how so to let go of their own fears and opinions that they could delight in each other honestly and openly. There would also be the whiff of the numinous in worship and the care of others so that heaven seemed to be just behind a thin veil. It would also be a community where creation hadn't been forgotten and where its corporate vocation included being priests for the world. But all this is idealistic language and perhaps consequently naïve and unbelievable. Then again, a kingdom whose charter is the Beatitudes has always struck me as improbable. God, it would seem, wants us to strive for that which seems absurd and foolish.

Yet, I think there can be moments when churches may come close to realizing a vision like this and thereby briefly point people toward a higher love and to a more abundant life. In my former congregation in North Carolina, I can remember times when the people were so closely united in love and fellowship, when they were actively giving of time and energy to the poor and needy, when everyone could depend absolutely on each other, when many of them worked together to love and instruct our children, and when worship were times of gentle joy that came close to such love. But these are often rare moments in the long life of congregations; they need to be encouraged and fostered all the same if for no other reason than to keep our churches from becoming too complacent or settling for anything less than sharing in the free delight of God's love for the world. So, as with individuals, the final stage can remain a guiding aspiration, a North Star to keep congregations striving and stretching in the right direction. Who knows? Perhaps God in his grace and mercy will give you and those in your care occasional glimpses of his eternal love and delight. I sincerely hope so.

I've taken turns in this short book to write about the ministry in light of God's generosity, freedom, delight, and love. But, of course, they're all one. They only seem different to us fallen human beings who have largely forgotten what each of them is. To be generous is to be free and to be truly free is to have discovered true love and delight. All are constantly offered to you in your ministry. Don't lose sight of that. A ministry that becomes so onerous that the palpable joy of God seems alien is a ministry that will likely lead to burnout and bitter feelings. Admittedly, the bureaucratic church has done much to overburden its clergy with regulations, meetings, paperwork, and periodic reviews so that a vocation can easily become dreary. The reform of those church regulations and expectations that drag the conduct of ministry away from being stewards of God's delight is arguably one of the most pressing needs of the church. How can we possibly show the world what it means to be stewards of delight and members of a new creation if our ministers are trapped in offices and meeting rooms with little opportunity or scope for pastoral ministry? How can they even begin to imagine what it might mean to be stewards if they are pressed into conforming to the bureaucratic needs of a late modern organization?

God has called us to be stewards of his love, his delight, and his generosity and freedom. To be a member of God's kingdom means among other things that our own individual and corporate lives participate in the abundant life of which these qualities are central. That's what it means to live within the life of Christ and what it means to have been redeemed. I'll even go so far as to say that we proclaim the gospel only insofar as we proclaim God's love, delight, generosity, and freedom. Salvation is never an escape to heaven at the end of our earthly lives but something we are given now within the community of the church and that impacts the world in which the church finds itself. By seeking to be stewards of God's delight, the royal priesthood of an inaugurated new creation, and the wooers of the estranged for a loving God who delights in all, we can manifest salvation to all around us. The people we meet in our daily lives desperately need that generous and delightful love—a love that will grant them freedom from darkness and despair. Indeed, a world that groans beneath the unremitting injury inflicted by our unsustainable living and insatiable appetites urgently needs us to reclaim that higher calling. So, make sure in your prayers and devotions that you immerse yourself deeply in God's endless love so that you all but vanish as that love flows out of your words and actions into those you encounter. Allow the God of love, delight, generosity, and freedom to work through you and then be amazed at what he can accomplish in your ministry.

Augustine famously began his *Confessions* by declaring, "You stir man to delight in praising you, because you made us for yourself, and our heart is restless until it rests in you."[13] The world is filled with restless, wandering hearts. Go out into that world in the company of the saints to bring them God's delight and love, which is the new creation of which we who are members of Christ's body are signs. Recover, inasmuch as God allows you, the Genesis ideal of serving as a member of God's priesthood, bearing his image by sharing in his delight for all creation and lifting creation's praise to God through your prayer and worship. Become a steward of his boundless delight by nurturing what is true, good, and beautiful and by challenging everything that seeks to make the world ugly through exploitation and abuse. In short, be a minister of the new creation by offering yourself wholly to God so that Christ may in you and through you draw others into the eternal and generous love of the Trinity. To be faithful stewards in whom Christ can be encountered is our highest calling, our deepest identity, and our greatest delight.

13. Augustine, *Confessions* 1.1.1.

Bibliography

Aelred of Reivaulx. *The Mirror of Charity*. Translated by Elizabeth Connor. Kalamazoo, MI: Cistercian, 1990.

————. *Spiritual Friendship*. Translated by Mary Eugenia Laker. Kalamazoo, MI: Cistercian, 1974.

Andrewes, Lancelot. "Sermon XIV." In vol. 3 of *Ninety-six Sermons by the Right Honourable and Reverend Father in God, Lancelot Andrewes, Sometime Lord Bishop of Winchester*, 3–22. Oxford: John Henry Parker, 1841.

Anonymous. "Wanderer." http://www.anglo-saxons.net/hwaet/?do=get&type=text&id=wdr.

Anselm. "Monologion." In *Anselm of Canterbury, The Major Works*, edited by Brian Davies and G. R. Evans, 3–81. Oxford: Oxford University Press, 1998.

————. "Proslogion." In *Anselm of Canterbury, The Major Works*, edited by Brian Davies and G. R. Evans, 4–104. Oxford: Oxford University Press, 1998.

Aquinas, Thomas. *On the Truth of the Catholic Faith: Summa contra Gentiles*. Translated by Anton C. Pegis. Garden City: Image, 1955.

————. *The Summa Theologica of St. Thomas Aquinas*, Vol. 1. New York: Benzinger Brothers, 1947.

Augustine of Hippo. *Commentary on the Lord's Sermon on the Mount with Seventeen Related Sermons*. Translated by David S. Kavanagh. Washington, DC: The Catholic University of America Press, 1951.

————. *Confessions*. Translated by Henry Chadwick. Oxford: Oxford University Press, 1991.

————. *Exposition of the Psalms 1–32*, III/15. Translated by Maria Boulding. Hyde Park, NY: New City, 2000.

————. *The Literal Meaning of Genesis*. In *On Genesis: On Genesis, A Refutation of the Manichees, Unfinished Literal Commentary on Genesis, The Literal Meaning of Genesis* I/13, translated by Edmund Hill, 153–506. Hyde Park, NY: New City, 2000.

————. *On the Trinity*. Edited by John E. Rotelle. Translated by Edmund Hill. Hyde Park, NY: New City, 1991.

————. *Sermons*, III/5 (148–183), "On the New Testament." Translated by Edmund Hill. Hyde Park, NY: New City, 1992.

————. *Unfinished Literal Commentary on Genesis*. In *On Genesis: On Genesis: A Refutation of the Manichees, Unfinished Literal Commentary on Genesis, The Literal Meaning of Genesis* I/13, translated by Edmund Hill, 103–51. Hyde Park, NY: New City, 2000.

Beale, Gregory K. "Eden, the Temple, and the Church's Mission in the New Creation." *JETS* 48.1 (2005) 5–31.

Bernard of Clairvaux. *Bernard of Clairvaux, A Lover Teaching the Way of Love: Selected Spiritual Writings*. Edited by M. Basil Pennington. New York: New City, 1997.

————. "On Loving God." In *Bernard of Clairvaux: Selected Words*, translated by G. R. Evans, 173–205. Classics of Western Spirituality. Mahwah, NJ: Paulist, 1987.

Bianco da Siena. "Come down, O love divine." http://cyberhymnal.org/htm/ c/o/comelove.htm.

Boersma, Hans. *Heavenly Participation: The Weaving of a Sacramental Tapestry*. Grand Rapids: Eerdmans, 2011.

Bonaventure. "The Life of St. Francis." In *Bonaventure: The Soul's Journey into God, The Tree of Life, The Life of St. Francis*, translated by Ewert Cousins, 177–327. Classics of Western Spirituality. Mahwah, NJ: Paulist, 1978.

————. "The Soul's Journey into God." In *Bonaventure: The Soul's Journey into God, The Tree of Life, The Life of St. Francis*, translated by Ewert Cousins, 52–116. Classics of Western Spirituality. Mahwah, NJ: Paulist, 1978.

Cavanaugh, William T. *Being Consumed: Economics and Christian Desire*. Grand Rapids: Eerdmans, 2008.

Chesterton, G. K. *Orthodoxy: The Romance of Faith*. New York: Image, 1959.

Dante Alighieri. *The Divine Comedy Vol. III: Paradise* ["Paradiso"]. Translated by Mark Musa. London: Penguin, 1984.

Delio, Ilia. *Simply Bonaventure: An Introduction to His Life, Thought and Writings*. Hyde Park, NY: New City, 2001.

Donne, John. "Sonnet 14." http://www.poetryfoundation.org/poem/173362.

The Episcopal Church. *Book of Common Prayer and Administration of the Sacraments and Other Rites and Ceremonies of the Church*. New York: Oxford University Press, 1928.

Ford, David F. *The Shape of the Living: Spiritual Directions for Everyday Life*. Grand Rapids: Baker, 1997.

Fortunatus, Venantius. "Salve, festa dies." http://www.oremus.org/hymnal/h/ h029.html.

Francis of Assisi. "Canticle of the Sun." In *Francis and Clare: The Complete Works*, edited by Regis L. Armstrong and Ignatius Brady. Mahwah, NJ: Paulist, 1982.

Hauerwas, Stanley. "What's love got to do with it? The politics of the cross." *Religion & Ethics*, April 5, 2012. http://www.abc.net.au/religion/articles/ 2012/04/05/3471386.htm

Herbert, George. "The Elixir." http://www.ccel.org/h/herbert/temple/Elixir.

———. "Love (III)." http://www.ccel.org/h/herbert/temple/Love3.html.

———. "Providence." http://www.ccel.org/h/herbert/temple/Providence.html.

Hopko, Thomas. *Orthodox Faith, vol. 2: Worship.* https://oca.org/orthodoxy/
the-orthodox-faith/worship/the-church-year/holy-saturday

Iacapone da Todi. "Of the Incarnation of the Divine Word." In *Penguin Book of
Italian Verse,* edited by George R. Kay, 13–17. Harmondsworth: Penguin,
1958.

Julian of Norwich. *The Showings of Julian of Norwich.* A Norton Critical Edition.
Edited by Denise N. Baker. New York: W. W. Norton, 2005.

Leech, Kenneth. *True Spirituality: An Introduction to Christian Spirituality.*
London: Sheldon, 1980.

Lewis, C. S. *Letters to Malcolm Chiefly on Prayer.* New York: Harvest, 1964.

———. *Miracles: A Preliminary Study.* New York: Simon and Schuster, 1960.

———. *The Problem of Pain.* London: HarperCollins, 1940.

Moltmann, Jürgen. *God in Creation: An Ecological Doctrine of Creation: The
Gifford Lectures 1984–1985.* Norwich: SCM, 1986.

Ramsey, Michael. *The Gospel and the Catholic Church.* London: Longmans,
1956.

Richard of St. Victor. *On the Trinity.* In *Trinity and Creation: Victorine Texts in
Translation: Exegesis, Theology and Spirituality from the Abbey of St Victor,*
translated by Hugh Feiss, 178–382. Hyde Park, NY: New City, 2011.

Sommerfeldt, John R. *Aelred of Reivaulx: On Love and Order in the World and
in the Church.* New York: Newman, 2006.

Tolkien, J. R. R. *The Letters of J. R. R. Tolkien.* Edited by Humphrey Carpenter.
Boston: Houghton Mifflin, 1981.

Traherne, Thomas. *Centuries.* New York: Harper and Brothers, 1960.

———. "Eden." http://www.poetryfoundation.org/poem/174680.

William of St. Thierry. *The Nature of Dignity of Love.* Translated by Thomas X.
Davis. Kalamazoo, MI: Cistercian , 1981.

Williams, Rowan. "Changing the Myths We Live By." In *Faith in the Public
Square,* 175–84. London: Bloomsbury, 2012.

———. *Tokens of Trust: An Introduction to Christian Belief.* Norwich:
Canterbury, 2007.

Wright, Tom. *The Challenge of Jesus: Rediscovering Who Jesus Was and Is.*
Downers Grove, IL: InterVarsity, 1999.

Printed in Great Britain
by Amazon.co.uk, Ltd.,
Marston Gate.